In Bed with the Enemy

Published by Parapress Ltd. 2002

Parapress Ltd.
The Basement
9 Frant Road
Tunbridge Wells
Kent
TN2 5SD

www.parapress.co.uk

ISBN: 1-898594-77-5

Illustrations by Andy Seldon
of Graham-Cameron Illustration

Illustrations on pp. 13, 15 and 25 by Harriet Buckley

Typset in Rezin and Utopia

British Library Catalogue-in-Publication Data:

A catalogue record of this book is available
from the British Library

In Bed with the Enemy

by

Aubrey Malone

with illustrations by Andy Seldon

PARAPRESS
LIMITED

Parapress has endeavoured to identify the correct originator of every quotation in this book. If any of the quotations are attributed in error the publishers would welcome all corrections and amendments for re-print.

Contents

The real thing

Hell hath no fury like a woman searching for a new lover.
(Cyril Connolly)

I had had enough. I couldn't take it anymore. It had been too many years since *Love Story*. I could feel all the goose-pimples coming out again. One night in a dream I thought I saw Joyce's Dollymount vision come home to roost. We were holding hands on the Hill of Howth, discussing the imperviousness of passion. 'You can have your existentialism and your smoggy streets,' she said to me, 'I want sultans on steamy sands.' 'But where will I get them?' I asked in my innocence, 'all we have today is smut and violence.' 'There is a way,' she said, drawing me close, 'just … one way.' 'Tell me about it!' I roared, my breath coming in pants now. 'Mills & Boon, Mills & Boon, Mills & Boon …'

I had heard of them all right, God knows who hadn't. But would I be good enough? I knew all about the stringent standards they expected, nay, deserved. Would I measure up? There was only one way to find out. An invisible power seemed to be pushing me onwards, willing me to make that vital phone call, to write that vital letter.

It became so powerful after a while I didn't even bother resisting it. I let the spirit guide me. I felt myself carried along almost by levitation. I was terrified … but excited too. It was like a divine presence inside me, pointing me to my destination. My head was muzzy, my legs were like jelly. But I still sat down at my rolltop. I took out my machine and set down the immortal words: 'One day I will write for Mills & Boon … .' As I looked at what I had written it seemed now more than ever clear to me that all my life heretofore had been an approximation towards this one moment, this epiphany. As I folded the piece of paper away inside an envelope I felt the Muse entering my soul. It said 'You will one day be rich and fulfilled … rich and fulfilled … fulfilled and rich …' I waited for more, but nothing came. Was it the voice of God? Was it my publisher? I tore my hair out in a kind of abstract rage; I felt possessed. Maybe this monster inside me was more than I could handle, maybe one day it would gear me towards a destructive, monstrous act … But I couldn't think about that now, I had to write, to write anything. I felt the rush of blood pounding inside my head as the words came tumbling out.

She squeezed his hand tightly and knew this time it was for real. What matter that he had no prospects – no English even! Her adoration was enough for both of them, enough for anything! She would throw in her job at the call centre and go with him to Peru. The more she thought about it, the more her parents' disapproval of him dissolved into thin air. She thought of all the years of artifice, of entertaining, of exchanging platitudes

with rajahs at exotic mansions. It was all like a bad dream now – replaced by her new fantasy – Leonardo!

His cold blue eyes looked through her piercingly and she shivered – as though in an ice-floe. But a moment later she was tremulous in his arms, she could feel the beads of sweat breaking out of every pore.

'Take me,' she whispered, biting his ear, 'take me now.' He needed no second invitation. He slid his hand up under her dress and unclasped her brassiere. She felt herself become drowsy, beginning to drown in his rosy hue. 'I'm yours,' she said in a daze, 'yours forever …' From a far-away part of herself she felt his ecstasy squeeze into her, exploding inside her, becoming one with her.

She dug her nails hard into his back until it bled and wailed gently. 'Let's stay like this forever,' he murmured, 'nothing matters except this.' He snuggled up beside her and she swooned again, like a little death. Her mind was gone from her now, her pleasure almost unbearable. 'No!' she shrieked as he groped her a moment later, 'I can't. If you do it to me again I will die, surely.'

'Then let us die together!' he moaned, taking her up in his arms and carrying her to the master bedroom.

I looked at the page for a long time, not fully believing I had actually written it myself. It was what I had been waiting my whole life to achieve, this noumenal self. With a trembling hand I took it out of my machine and put it into an envelope. There was only one more thing to be done before sending it off – I would listen once more to tape that the Mills & Boon agents had sent me, on how to write for them. I had already played it a dozen times, but even that wasn't enough. I turned off the light and closed my eyes as the words wafted into the innards of my soul.

Chapter 1
Quest

If she looks old, she's old. If she looks young she's young.
If she looks back, follow her.

(Bob Hope)

The really real thing

Love is two minutes and fifty-two seconds
of squishing noises.

(Johnny Rotten)

No matter how many advances there are in medical technology, this four-lettered word l-o-v-e, or what passes for it among the minds of the myopic or infatuated, will continue to be the name of the most incurable disease this planet contains. And as many people will continue to be as much in love with the ideal as with their often obscure objects of desire.

Somerset Maugham called it; 'a dirty trick played by God to achieve continuation of the species'. Jerome K. Jerome, of *Three Men in a Boat* fame, believed it was like the measles – everyone went through it. Judith Viorst was somewhat kinder. She said love is much nicer to be in than an 'automobile accident, a tight corset, a high tax bracket, or a holding pattern over Philadelphia'.

Mae West, who ought to have known about such things, believed love could conquer all things 'except poverty and toothache'. But then, when you're in love, who cares about such trivia as toothaches and money? Writer Lynda Barry compared it to 'an exploding cigar we willingly ignite'. Lord Wavell, pursuing the cigar metaphor, commented 'If it goes out you can light it again, but it never quite tastes the same'. Actor John Barrymore said it was 'that delightful moment between meeting a girl and discovering she looks like a haddock'. Charming.

Seriously, though, what is it about this intangible thing that makes us act like a gibbering idiot when we can be the epitome of practicality and decorum in every other walk of life? Maurice Chevalier once said, 'Many a man has fallen in love with a girl in a light so dim he wouldn't have chosen a suit by it.' And married her too, it would seem. The difference with a suit, however, is that you can give it back. And you don't have to pay it alimony every month either.

In one of her novels Françoise Sagan wrote, 'Every little girl knows about love. It is only her capacity to suffer because of it that increases as she grows up.' Ditto for every little boy. The main reason for this, of course, is that when

---

If love is the answer, would you mind
rephrasing the question?
(Lily Tomlin)

---

we're young we read stories that end, almost inevitably, with those six magical words 'and they lived happily ever after'. We're never told the secret of how Cinders and Prince Charming preserved their devotion to each other. We're told, baldy that they just did. It's very neat way to end a story. You read a hundred plus pages about a love that blossomed passionately over a few weeks ... and then not a sausage about the next fifty years. Curious.

What I'm wondering is how someone like Cinderella would feel if her prince came home one night legless? Did they never have arguments about things like who'd put out the bins? What would happen if they were a few quid short one month with his mortgage repayments on the castle? Would she have taken a night job cleaning to help out? And more to the point: what happens when she realises that Prince Charming has promised to make Sleeping Beauty live happily ever after as well? See: even fairytale husbands cheat.

For those of you who haven't made it to the fairytale castle, do not fear, help is at hand. Hopefully this book will be your guide to that most delicate of beasts. It's for when another Saturday night has come and gone and you haven't stepped outside the house. For when another four hours has been spent sitting by the phone waiting for that Cute Thing you met at that club to ring. He looked sincere, he sounded sincere, but when you think about it, that's right, he was like All The Rest. A man involved in a lifelong love affair with … himself.

You don't want to spend the rest of your life alone, so what do you do? Risk being humiliated at the same club next weekend? Give a tinkle to that nice-but-dull sod that's being haranguing you for the last six months? Try the friend-of-a-friend-of-a-friend that might (but probably won't) be your soulmate?

Or even, God love us, put an ad in the classified pages?

The playing field

Meeting someone is quite a complex business. Nobody seems to know what they're looking for. Personally I'm the strong silent type, but that's only because I find it difficult to talk and suck my beer gut in at the same time. Most people aren't as simple as me however and I have to admit that I'm intensely confused. First we had the Old

Man. Then came the New Man, who wasn't macho or aggressive. He doesn't come across all flash and cocky or have tattoos or wear medallions or insist on taking his girlfriend to heavy metal concerts. He's shy, taciturn and loves pushing the pram around the supermarket. But somehow women still weren't satisfied with this reformed character and the New Old Man appeared in response. He was slightly less macho and full of himself than the Old

Man, but equally wasn't a wimp either. But the New Man wasn't to be outdone and, you've guessed it, the Old New Man arrived on the scene. The penultimate phenomenon, I'm told (I don't get out much, you see) is the New Lad, who's kind of Old New Man mixed up with a bit of the New Old Man.

We haven't had a New New Man yet, but the old Old Man is still there lurking about even if he won't admit it. Which is precisely the thing, I think. Many so-called New Men are really Old Men in disguise, using their newness as a kind of sophisticated foreplay – to attract New Women … who may well be Old Women pretending to be New Women so they can attract the Old Men pretending to be the New Men.

Are you still following? Worst of all is the latest female to hit the Sunday supplements. This, in case you haven't been reading your papers, is the Ladette. The Ladette is feminism's answer to the lad … or is she? While true-blue feminists have been busting a gut on the Real Issues (the right to choose, equal pay for equal work, etc.) ladettes have their own definition of equality of the sexes: the right to drink themselves stupid and fall out of taxis at 3 a.m. with their left leg hooked round their right ear as they barf into the gutter like their male predecessors in the lager lout department.

Is this dumbing down to the male level actual liberation or merely another form of enslavement? If women truly want to go down this road, we will no doubt end up with even more dysfunctionality in the world than we have already, so the cure is worse than the disease. On the other hand, if the drunk Old Men see the New Women getting as legless as them, they might take a long hard look at themselves and realise where they've been going wrong. If such an eventuality transpires, we might see a

new generation of reconstructed males terrified of reconstructed females. Take this scenario to its logical conclusion and you'd have a future where we'd still have our quota of yobbos, but now they're women.

I'm sure it must have been easier when we were all neanderthals. Stone Age man just went around hitting women on the head with clubs and dragging them back to his cave. Which was fine until the women started hitting back. It's a good thing Wilma Flintstone didn't think of this or she'd have turned Fred into a New Man. He might have thrown away his club and started eating tofu.

Stone Age men and women do have to be excused for having aggressive tendencies because they didn't have all the creature comforts we do. They couldn't go down to Marks and Spencer for their condoms, for instance, or write to agony aunts if their marriage went pear-shaped. Neither did they have the facility of silicon implants, liposuction or collagen injections to make themselves desirable for that Saturday night jamboree.

But they also didn't have to put up with the 'you really

aren't listening to me' line. If a Stone Age woman said 'Nguiphamo opsjbgksjgsakj dkjsbkjfb isajlkhdb' for instance, who was to know what she really meant was 'I'm suffering from PMT at the minute so excuse me if I have to fake my orgasms'? Her partner meanwhile, had to do without vasectomies, internet sex and *Playboy* centre-folds. Mind you it's not all bad, he wouldn't have had Germaine Greer yammering on about the phenomeno-logy of sexual politics so maybe it all pans out.

They also didn't have Linda Lovelace, Alfred Kinsey or Marie Stopes. They didn't have John and Yoko love-ins, new Age-y group hugs or Rohypnol. Life was much simpler when you didn't have to worry about lesbian rights activists chaining themselves to pillars if you said something unPC. People were far too busy bonking pterodactyls over the head to worry about the nuances of sexual politics. But I'm sure the more pro-active feminists of the time organised Montessori creches for their fledg-lings while they went of to work gathering in the nuts and berries. And the ones who didn't look like Raquel Welch in *One Million Years BC* probably burned their furry bras, smacking rocks together to make fire.

I don't think I'm really getting anywhere with all this so excuse me while I go and do the ironing. After that I have to do some babysitting and put some clothes on the line like any self-respecting old Old Man trying his best to appear like a New Old one. I wonder if my old man – sorry, father – ever had problems like this? Or was he too busy shifting pints of the Black Stuff in the ginmill to care?

Unfortunately for us, since my old man's day, a new Stone Age woman has emerged, namely Sharon. An ice-pick may not be a match for a club; but if it ever came to a tussle between Ms Stone and dear old Fred, I can tell you who my money would be on.

16

In short, the battle of the sexes goes on. As Margaret Mead once said, 'Women want mediocre men ... and men are trying to be as mediocre as possible.' Mae West's take on the subject was, 'Some women pick men to marry – and some others pick them to pieces.' Which isn't to say that the war is one-sided. A judge in the Old Bailey some time ago threw a rape case out of court with the comment 'When women say no they don't always mean no. Men can't turn their emotions on and off like a tap as some women can.' I think Joan Collins put her finger on it: 'All men are rats – and those who aren't are boring.'

All this leaves us in a rather confused state. But, while we men are completely baffled by what women think they want us to want to be like, we can take some solace in the fact that women are all equally baffled. Women can't understand why all the forward men are bastards and the nice ones are shy or have no money. While the ones that do are gay. Nobody is going to get what they want in this crapshoot called love. If the man in your life has every-thing you want, then he probably won't want you, which of course will make you want him more.

The answer would be to meet in the middle. He's not perfect as looks go and neither is he going to threaten Bill Gates with his bank account but he'll do in a push. Better get that pre-nup, though! From his point of view, as soon as you show any interest at all, he'll probably go all cold on you, like all men.

The best policy is to play the waiting game, make him work his butt off to woo you and then casually tell him you might be interested in that romantic weekend for two in Paris that he's forking out for ... if you haven't anything more interesting on.

Above all, remember Oscar Wilde's advice – 'She who hesitates is won'.

17

Man hunting

A woman never pursues a man – but then a mousetrap doesn't pursue a mouse either.

(Ronnie Barker)

Most women are looking for Mr Right – if not Mr Goodbar. But where to find him? And what would he look like?

There are many books out there that try to give pointers. Except that they don't tell you about Mr Right so much as Mr Wrong. I suppose the logic is that if you weed out all the Mr Wrongs, you'll eventually come upon Mr Will Do, Mr Half-Right, if not Ben Affleck and Benito del Toro rolled into one. So there's hope for us all.

However this somewhat assumes that women know what they're looking for in a man in the first place. In a recent voxpop survey (so, yes, it *was* a fair selection of female society as a whole, or at least the ones who were outside the Odeon that night) girls almost always said 'a sense of humour'. Which is becoming increasingly difficult with the pint being priced out of existence and men being bashed for just about everything that's wrong in the world.

The next thing that popped out was 'personality'. Quite what personality is seems to be a bit of a mystery, even to the girls who said it. For me personality means you're 'one of the lads'. Which usually means going out, getting horrendously drunk, dancing erratically for a couple of hours, have a scrap with some poor unsuspecting bugger and waking up the next morning not having any recollection of what happened.

A third favourite was 'a good mixer'. Not to be confused

with what you put in your whiskey to delay the inevitable drunkenness and reduce the chances of vomiting. The other interpretation is that you're capable of chatting up all her mates. This strikes me as an invitation to the green-eyed monster to come and perch on the girl's shoulder, but hey, if it's what she wants.

The final thing that emerged, usually towards to the end of their 30-second interview was 'tall, dark and handsome'. Which just goes to show, looks may not be everything, but they're the only thing that makes sense.

However, it's very rare that a woman actually gets to decide what men are going to be like. They tend to come pre-packaged and pre-programmed. Men come in many shapes and sizes, and here are just a few of them.

People to meet no. 1: The Yuppy

Familiarity breeds, and when you spend most of your life around the office it's not unreasonable to expect one of your co-workers to take a shine to you at some point. The species most prevalent in such places of employ are alpha males terrified of showing their true selves (like most men in the world) which is why they dress to kill and pepper their conversation with rent-a-cliché soundbites.

What's really going on is a quasi-sophisticated version of the 'Me Tarzan You Jane' game in a yuppy environment. Strip away the Armani suit, the state-of-the-art laptop and the mobile phone and what have you got? That's right: Stone Age man looking to club the nearest unsuspecting female.

To combat him, you've got to fight like with like. If he's Donald Trump, you can be Ivana. Let's remember that Ivana came out with the maxim that every woman should have in her armoury when it comes to the battle of the sexes: 'Don't get mad, get everything'.

Here in any case are some of the identifying characteristics of *Yuppieus latterdayibus*:

Dresses: In anything by Jean-Paul Gaultier.
Breeding Habits: Nocturnal.
Nests: Pinstripesuitland, All Bar One, Leafy Suburbs.
Drives: BMW, Saab, Peugeot.
Likes: Leggy bimbos who work for computer firms.
Speaks: Ersatz mid-Atlantic drawl.
Reads: Tomes shortlisted for the Booker Prize (and Jackie Collins)
Listens to: Pavarotti (and Destiny's Child).
Pet hates: Bohemian intellectuals and pinkos.
Politics: Dubaya Bush.
Sex fantasies: Kathy Lloyd, Kate Winslet and Kelly Brook.
Vices: Gucci watches, Gucci shoes, cellular phone.
Ambitions: To run the country or, failing that, to own an island.
Can be spotted: At all the best hostelries, in season.
Hobbies: Windsurfing, being bitchy about friends.
Socialises: Anywhere there's an unidentified cliché flying around.
Plays: Golf (badly) and paintball (well).
Drinks: Pints of proper real ale, none of that lager stuff.
Greets friends: 'Hi y'all', 'Hi you guys' and variations of.
Chat-up line: 'You faxed a letter for me, hon'.
Works: As a middle manager in data processing firm.
Migrates: Ibiza, the Algarve and the Seychelles.
Biggest fear: Midlife crisis, or an original thought.
Best before: Publication of *Bonfire of the Vanities*.
Projected extinction date: 2006, except in some areas of London and New York where populations are expected to continue to thrive.

People to meet no. 2: The Secret Admirer

Are you on the receiving end of a Grand Passion? Is your letterbox clogged tight with billets-doux every February 14? More to the point, how many of these are signed and how many of the Secret Admirer variety?

I've always been a bit fazed about secret admirers. I mean, if you like someone, why keep it under wraps? Secret Despisers I can understand – we call it hate mail. But anonymous love mail? The admirer, presumably, goes through hell because of his/her passion. The admiree on the other hand, tears her hair out wondering where the (probably scented) missive came from.

Could it be that pimply adolescent I see at the bus stop every morning? Or is it that dishy executive that just moved upstairs? This sort of thing could drive a body to distraction. Another question is, how many of these Romeos – either anonymous or acknowledged – can you trust? If you're in the throes of a Magnificent Obsession at the moment, or are interested in getting involved in one, you should be aware of the dangers of putting all your eggs in the one bastard. Secret Admirers like to think that they are quite noble characters who enjoy the looking from afar and being an unrequited love. He imagines himself to be a Lancelot, a knight-errant denied his Queen.

However, if you manage to get out on a date with him you may find yourself in a place with soft lights and plenty of muzak. Before long he'll discover whether you live alone or not. This will be divined by a casual aside. There will be little or no suggestiveness in his voice, though if you live with your family it's bye-bye time. While this subtle inquisition is going on you'll find him interesting and charming while he'll find out every detail of your life. He'll consume no more than two or three drinks before he starts his assault. He doesn't need much Dutch courage.

He'll then inform you he's off his food, that he can't sleep at night, that you're his sole reason for living. Despite your internal crap detector you'll be sucked in by his boyish charm. Flattery gets Romeo absolutely everywhere.

And now you find out why he decided to remain a 'Secret' Admirer for so long. If he leaves early he's either going home to his mum or to his wife. If not he's probably a groper, or worse. Gradually drawing you in until you can't say no. To prepare yourself for this moment we recommend investigating the wide range of self-defence weapons available from American catalogues. The taser is our personal favourite, just don't test it out on your dog first.

People to meet no. 3: The Clubber

Okay girls, here are a few guidelines you might care to bear in mind in getting involved with that species known as *Bachelorous rovingus* who you may run into if you decide to go clubbin'. Or at least how to recognise him. He'll be called something like Tony, Joe, Des, Jimmy, Dave, Frank … in fact anything nondescript and forgettable. Nine times out of ten these are pseudonyms (*Bachelorus rovingus* doesn't usually have the imagination to make up an uncommon made-up name). He'll be dapper, well-built, and could loosely be described as handsome. Not as handsome as he thinks himself, though. (He's the type that walks down the side of the street that has the most windows in which he can admire himself). When he gets you into a corner he'll begin his 'smouldering' routine which he's probably practised in the mirror for at least half an hour before he came out. This usually involves undressing you with his irresistible baby blue eyes. It will go on until you either fall headlong for him or decide to practice your kickboxing.

His job will sound very interesting, if you can hear him over the music, that is. What he doesn't tell you is that his job title will be something like Senior Administrative Assistant. Sometimes this consists of trips to the continent on Extremely Urgent PR junkets. You'll be honoured with details of these trips periodically and expected to listen attentively as he continues his tirade well into the night. If you have a super-intelligent question to ask he may deign to allow you to interrupt his monologue.

On the plus side he'll carry several different varieties of credit card, banker's card and cash card, possibly in a mini-filofax. While this may seem like a turn-off you can immediately translate all these things into money with which to make him pur-chase you drinks. He, of course, will think that getting you drunk is a quick way into your knickers. Unfortunately his self-image requires him to drink Guinness and a JD chaser for the Hard Man effect. He's also under the misapprehension that his constitution is bigger than yours, so as he

swills two drinks to your one all you have to do is wait until he falls over, thank him politely and wander off, having consumed your nightly allowance of alcohol gratis.

People to meet no. 4: The Wimp

You'll be having a quiet coffee in that nice little cafe across the road when you first notice him. He'll be deep in thought, wading through *War and Peace* or *Paradise Lost.* Over a few weeks you'll get used to his face, start smiling at him as you pass, admiring his intelligence and quiet sensitivity. And he's always so polite. You just know that he'll take you somewhere nice, like the theatre or opera if you give him the right signals. But beware! Remember that real men prefer beer to coffee and so Starbucks and Coffee Republic aren't going to be the usual destination for a normal red-blooded male. This character is called *Wimpus modernicus*; alone among his sex he does not 'hang out' in pubs or bars because ordering his favourite drink of a daiquiri is bound to get him beaten up.

Wimpus modernicus is a delicate creature who was most likely President of the Debating Team at school and became editor of the university rag paper. Sweetly articulate in all situations, he's known to actually listen when you speak, but only because he realises that this almost unique ability among men is his edge when it comes to scoring.

Politically speaking he defines himself as an 'incurable liberal', after which he grins coyly. In his spare time he's been known to work for Greenpeace and Save the Seal campaigns, although only because this highly-educated beast knows exactly how to tug on the heart-strings of an innocent and naïve young girl. To the same end, however, his major concern is the (s)exploitation of women by both the media and society, failing to recognise that Women's Lib happened in the 1970s and he's thirty years too late.

Though he doesn't smoke 'cancer sticks' himself – or anything else for that matter – he believes in the individual's right to choose. To this end, he believes cannabis should be legalised. He reached this frame of mind on his first holiday without his parents, the year he *nearly* got stoned.

Wimpus modernicus, as you might have gleaned by now, is the type of man any girl could bring home to her mother – though maybe not to her father. He may have spent more time reading D. H. Lawrence than dirt-back riding in the Hellfire Club himself, but he's ozone friendly – and ultra-trendy – enough for you not to notice. In yesteryear we would have called him yellow; today he gets away with green.

On the odd occasion he goes to the cinema he makes sure it's Robert Redford and not Sylvester Stallone. More likely than not he'll have long hair while in his garage will be a Harley Davidson … although only for effect. He does so hate getting his hands smudged with oil.

If you spend time with *Wimpus modernicus* you'll notice he never leaves the toilet seat up or the toothpaste out of the tube. He showers three times and day and fantasises about getting a jacuzzi if and when he gets 'kicked upstairs' at work.

His one domestic fault is the fact that he keeps all his unmatching socks in a special drawer in the perennial hope that one day he'll luck out and find two unmatching ones that match each other (try to get excited as he tells you this – it means so much to the little dear).

His favourite approach to women is the little-boy-lost one. He regularly scours *Cosmo* and *Glamour* for other inside information about how they like to be approached.

Wimpus modernicus is the man best able to make articulate, slightly cheeky jokes at wedding receptions but still get on with eighty-three-year-old aunt Ethel. If and when he gets married himself his relationship will be one of 'sharing' and he may well become a househusband some day. So great is the guy's empathy with the female condition he'll all but suffer PMT alongside you – if not post-natal depression as well. Because that's what you really need in a household with a new baby – two parents not being at their best! He'll always be there for you, as they say in the American soaps, and will never make any fuss about sharing wash-up duties, or babysitting while you go to your Tupperware party (in fact he'll even be peeved off about missing this).

On the debit side, he'll earwig conversations if you're having one of your 'girlie' evenings with friends, and sometimes might even chip in his ten cents worth, to the chagrin of all present who'd prefer him to do what a man's gotta do at such times – get the hell out of the living-room and into the kitchen to shake the cocktails. To some he may appear more like a candidate for an Adam and Steve relationship rather than an Adam and Eve one, but he'll stick by you through thick and thin, even on those nights when you beg him to go down to the pub and get skulled.

This man, as I said, will definitely be present at the birth of your child. Do your best to ensure he's at the conception as well.

The party

The best place to find single men these days is in the frozen food department of the supermarket around seven p.m.
(Oprah Winfrey)

Apart from the frozen food aisle, a party is perhaps the most fertile ground for meeting people. Everyone is well lubricated, lusting to have a good time and wanting to see and be seen. However there are guaranteed to be some people whom you may prefer not to. Here's a shortlist of the most offensive species. As is the case with a disease, identifying them early can facilitate prevention, which is always better than cure.

The Smoocher

He wants to sing 'sensitive' Chris de Burgh numbers all night long on his spanking new geetar. When he walks in he deposits it on the centre of the floor like the eighth wonder of the world. He invites himself up of the rostrum and proceeds to mouth (out of tune) every bar of the most tendentious muzak de Burgh ever penned. Boobytraping the mike is the only way to stop him – or, if all else fails, take his guitar away from him and start where he left off. Thereafter the rest of the revellers can take the cotton wool out of their ears.

They've put a man on the moon, now let's get the rest of them up there.
(Kathy Lette)

The Hooplehead

This man is the last of the red-hot hippies. His mind has been out to lunch since about 1988. He did an MA in philosophy that year and since then has been walking the streets of London reading Rimbaud, signing on, and applying to do social work. He thinks he should be running the country, despite the fact he couldn't run a bath. He's also got another slight problem: he finds it hard to work up the enthusiasm to get up in the morning.

He'll already be legless when he arrives at the party and will then proceed to drink himself sober. He realises his ambition at about 7 a.m., by which time he's flaked out on the sofa staring at the ceiling and attempting to recite Horace or Pliny in the original. Tread delicately on his dreams. Ask him politely if he'd like a cup of strong black coffee when he comes back to earth (or indeed if). Otherwise this type can be safely ignored.

The Berk from work

He hasn't the confidence to say boo to a goose all year but, fortified by alcohol, has managed to reveal himself without vomiting. He'll start acting like Oliver Reed on a bad night. In fact it's almost as bad as the office party last Christmas when he spent most of the time either insulting the boss or trying to photocopy his bum. First off he tells you he's adored you from the first time he clapped eyes on you but has never had the courage to tell you. A few Johnny Walkers later and he's sticking cocktail sausages up his nostrils and trying to put your goldfish into the microwave before passing out. You might feel sorry for him, the hopeless loser. Put him in a cold shower and ring his mum to ask her to come and pick him up.

The Depressive

He's supine on the stairs after throwing up his kebab all over the carpet. He's just been rejected by the love of his life and has decided to fling himself off the nearest bridge. He asks you what your life is all about. Don't get sucked in by the veneer of someone willing to listen to you instead of talking at you. You'll soon be listening to his own jaw-droppingly tortuous angst.

The Philanthropist

He wants to solve the problems of the Third World over liqueurs, but he wouldn't buy a copy of the *Big Issue* to save his life. Unfortunately these people come with no distinguishing marks so it's quite easy to get trapped. A sudden acute attack of diarrhoea may come in handy.

The Sexual Liberal

From very early on in the night he wants to put all the key-rings in a sack and whoever picks out a certain ring gets to drive that person's partner home. I suggest running. Fast.

---

*A girl can't wait for the right man to come along,
but in the meantime that still doesn't mean
that she can't have a wonderful time
with all the wrong ones.*
(Cher)

The Singer

This is a fellow without a note in his head who wants to do 'American Pie' – and I mean every verse (how is it that crows always have great memories?) Fortunately he'll have to engage in a scuffle with The Smoocher to get his hands on the mike. Sit back, relax and enjoy.

Avoiding these deadbeats sometimes doesn't give you much time to locate that Significant Other you're pining for. Don't let it get you down if all of your mates seemed to have managed it before you. If one of them tells you that her man is 'really sweet' the subtext reads: 'Extremely dull, but non-threatening and marginally better than nothing.' Similarly for 'I don't really like the glitzy type – I'm more of a video and chips girl' read: 'I wonder what he's going to do for a face once King Kong wants his arse back.'

---

*Mother: If I let you go to the party do you
promise to be good?
Daughter: I won't be just good, I'll be fantastic!*

Women aren't the only ones to perpetrate these lies to save face. Men are, if anything, more inventive. 'Her legs aren't the best part of her' implies a certain resemblance to tree trunks. 'She's put on a little weight' suggests she's eaten the EU grain mountain. 'She's seen better days' means she's unlikely to see worse ones. So if at first you don't succeed don't take it to heart – those that did may already be regretting it.

Return to slender

Diet is just die with a 't'

(Garfield)

While some people say looks are only s(k)in deep they're still important. And one of the most important things by which other people will instantly judge you is your weight. Oscar Wilde used to say that everything he liked was either illegal, immoral or fattening. I know the feeling.

Do you worry about your figure? Does the Pope pray?

But is there such a phenomenon as the 'ideal' diet? It would probably be easier to get to the dark side of the moon – or teach Jason Donovan to sing. As Peter Gray has it, 'Quite often, the part of the body to lose weight first in a fashionable diet is the brain'. And yet hardly a week goes by without some new earth – or avoirdupois – shattering tome on the subject. And the more outrageous, apparently, the better the sales. Because desperate situations (and shapes) require increasingly desperate remedies. Or at least would-be remedies. From my experience you'd be better off eating the pages of said tomes to quell your appetite than actually following their advice. What a waste of a perfectly good tree.

Syndicated satirist Erma Bombeck, mistress of the screwball one-liner, once said that, according to her girth, 'I should be a ninety-foot redwood'. I'm sure that's positively anorexic in comparison to some individuals who, either due to 'glandular problems' or an obsession with launching merciless offensives on those domestic appendages we call refrigerators each time they pass, can do little or nothing to stop themselves ballooning.

Chat show hostess extraordinaire Oprah Winfrey, for her squillions, can't come up (or should that be down?) with a diet that could solve her weight problem. Being an extremist by nature she seems able to muster her energies to combat the inch (possibly foot) pinch for short periods, but then pigs out and undoes in an afternoon what it has taken perhaps a month or more to achieve. 'I went on a two week diet once,' she quipped 'and all I lost was a fortnight.' And elsewhere: 'I eat when I'm depressed and I eat when I'm happy. When I can't decide if I'm depressed or happy I make the decision while I'm eating.' Laugh if you'll, but such comments strike me as emanations of someone who has thrown a towel over her problem.

Even more depressingly Serena Gray once described a woman as 'a diet waiting to happen,' and one would imagine the lion's share of diet books are directed towards females probably because society puts such prejudicially high premium on women with hour glass figures, and thus exacerbating such conditions as anorexia nervosa and bulimia. She also adds that if the average woman knew as much about sexual politics as she does about the number of calories in a piece of cheesecake, we would be living in a matriarchal society instead of a patriarchal one.

Brenda Fricker said that in *Raging Bull* when Robert de Niro put on all that poundage to play Jake La Motta he became hero-worshipped overnight by all the Method-orientated critics. But if she put on that much she'd probably be told by her agent to shape up or ship out. Which is why it was nice to see Renee Zellweger being praised for putting on a few pounds for *Bridget Jones' Diary* and being complimented on the way she looked.

Her hot pants were so tight I could hardly breathe.
(Benny Hill)

However, once back in the US she instantly dropped back to her stick-insect self. Which seems to be the way in America. Americans are often either grossly over- or under-weight, there's no in between. The under-weight ones tend to have superiority complexes, whereas their opposites are more, let us say, well-adjusted. In fact that's what this is really all about. Nobody wants to go out with someone who is obsessed with their weight. Equally nobody wants to go out with a whale.

Breaking the ice

Do you sleep on your stomach? Do you mind if I do?
(Anon.)

Once you've disposed of the all the people you don't wish to chat up or be chatted up by and have identified a likely target all you have to do is face that gut-wrenching, agonising moment of how to strike up a conversation. Of course the easiest way for a woman to do this is to bat her eyelashes and wait for the man to initiate. This tactic has been pioneered by the fairer sex for many centuries and until recently was their sole domain. For women it is embarrassingly easy to get noticed, provoking the man to make contact. However now that we now live in the 'naughties' (2000s) some men are getting confused and are copying their female colleagues in the waiting game. So now we have two groups of people staring at each other across the dance floor. Without the assets of cleavage and bum men are at a distinct disadvantage and more radical approaches are called for. Like language ... and preferably style.

Cheeky – and chauvinist – chat-up lines probably go back as far as the Garden of Eden ... except there it seems to be the female who was doing the wooing. As you know, it wasn't the apple on the tree, it was the pair on the ground. Unfortunately some chat-up lines have been around nearly as long, 'I must have met you in a previous life; I feel this karma drawing me towards you every time we meet' is more than likely to make the object of your desire break the Fifth Commandment.

Equally the old favourite and massively unoriginal 'Did it hurt when you fell – from heaven I mean?' is almost as toe-curlingly cringe-inducing as 'You must be tired – you've been running through my head all day'. Do people actually spend time dreaming up this BS? The reality of the matter is that women are all too well aware that the more elaborate the would-be pick-up line, the more likely its speaker is to be a total and utter plonker/nerd/berk/dimwit. And, almost certainly, a two-timing waste of space.

More daring individuals may wish to try 'Have I asked you to sleep with me yet? My memory is terrible.' Or, again as an opener to a perfect (or preferably imperfect) stranger: 'What would you like for breakfast?' The great Irish chat-up line is the immortal 'Would you like to be buried with my people?' Be extremely cautious using this one, it's actually a none-too-romantic marriage proposal. Another one is, 'It's easy to lie with a straight face, but more fun with a curved body.'

Hardened discomaniacs who don't even bother tucking their wedding rings into their lapel pockets can be guaranteed to come up with something along the lines of 'I'm very happily divorced' or 'My wife doesn't understand me' ... which really means 'My wife understands me too well.' While puns like 'If I said you had a beautiful body would you hold it against me?' may earn a laugh, or maybe just a thick ear.

Some men favour the brazen approach: 'Do you go for suave, sophisticated, filthy rich intellectuals with a great sense of humour and a bubbly personality? Or will you settle for me?' Hugh Hefner of the Playboy harem was once asked what his favourite chat-up line was and he replied: 'That's easy. My name is Hugh Hefner.' One suspects that this only works if you actually *are* Hugh Hefner though.

Of course if you can't be bothered with the interminable put-downs by haughty girls who simply laugh and stalk off, you could try the ultimate in cutting through all the red tape that goes with the dating game by simply asking: 'Will you marry me?' Now who could resist that?

Finding Mr Right

There's only one original thing about men, original sin.
(Helen Rowland)

There are several early warning signs that you've found that perfect someone. Your brain will leave on an extended holiday while your mouth adopts a constant smile. Your legs will become wobbly due to lack of blood circulation, being needed elsewhere, while the blank glare of your eyes show that, although the wheel is spinning, the hamster is most certainly dead. Hours (possibly weeks) will be wasted while you sit by the phone waiting for him to ring.

In men the signs are slightly different. They'll only look at other women when you're not around. They'll make a special effort to remember what you said ten minutes ago and start to notice the subtle differences in your hair and make-up since they last saw you. They may even comment on it and say how good you look. However, don't hold out for flowers because as Sophia Loren said 'when a man gives you flowers for no reason, there's always a reason'. Equally, if you have suspicions that he's got another girl on the go, don't confront him with it as he's likely to say 'Nothing happened' (meaning 'She wouldn't let me').

If you're worried that you've found someone but don't really know where you're going together as a couple here's how to tell if you should be hearing alarm bells instead of the wedding ones. 'To me it's not just about the sex' roughly translates to 'I think about nothing else *but* sex'. And if he mentions the two words 'open relationship' it's time to walk away.

Kissing

For a woman a kiss is the end of the beginning. For a man it's the beginning of the end.

(Helen Rowland)

Marilyn Monroe's view of kissing was that it felt good … but didn't last as long as a diamond tiara. Apart from this rather sceptical view, you'll be pleased to know that kissing is excellent exercise. Three minutes of passionate snogging burns up around 12 calories, which is about a thirtieth of a Mars bar – now there's a fitness regime! It also exercises twelve facial muscles, and keeps wrinkles at bay. This is of course a good chat-up line in itself – but choosing the right moment can be tricky, unless of course you're an Eskimo who rubs noses in case a bit of saliva freezes and acts like superglue in the sub-zero temperature.

Choosing the wrong moment can have alarming consequences as Thomas Saverland found out to his distress in 1837. Attempting to kiss his girlfriend he was quite surprised when she bit his nose off. He was understandably quite annoyed and took her to court. Unfortunately the judge agreed with her. 'When a man kisses a girl against her will', he said, 'she's fully entitled to bite his nose off if she so pleases.' Gents, you have been warned.

I am in favour of preserving the French habit of kissing ladies' hands – after all, one must start somewhere!

(Sacha Guitry)

Once you've obtained permission to kiss a girl you now have to get over the next hurdle. Apparently girls are beginning to go off French kissing with chaps that they don't know *très bien*. And, worse, zoologist Desmond Morris claims that the whole practice originated when mothers weaned their babies by chewing their food and passing it into their infants' mouths. So now when lovers explore each other's mouths with their tongues, they're really experiencing the primeval pleasure of a baby feed. No wonder girls are going off French kissing, thinks Desmond.

Kissing is as old as the human race but there are more ways to do it than the simple French Kiss. Suffice it to say that the old folk wisdom applies when one is giving advice about when to do it, how to do it, whether to do it and – most importantly – where to do it. One important thing to remember is that if a kiss speaks volumes, it's probably not a first edition. And it takes a lot of practice for a man to learn to kiss like a beginner.

---

*It takes a lot of experience for a girl to kiss
like a beginner.*
(Anon.)

There's also the eye question. According to researchers, 37% men kiss with their eyes open, while a whopping 97% of females keep theirs closed. The remaining 3% just get very annoyed when they find out you've kept your eyes open. Why? Is it cheating to look? A sort of voyeurism from within? Whatever the reason, girls don't like it and wise heads avoid arguments before they start.

A man should also note that a woman will remember her first kiss long after you've forgotten your last. And girls should remember that while kisses are nice they're often only a distraction while the man tries to undo your bra. Certainly Tony Curtis viewed them as a necessary evil. He said canoodling with Marilyn Monroe on the set of *Some Like it Hot* was 'like kissing Hitler'. Maybe he forgot to bring the tiara.

---

*The kiss is a wordless articulation of desire
whose object lies in the future, and somewhat
to the south.*
(Lance Morrow)

How to get out of going on a date

There are a lot more interesting things in life than sex.
Like gardening for instance.

(Jean Alexander)

So you've spent a few nights with him, your radar was on the blink as Cupid sent out a few poisoned arrows and now, in the cold light of day, you realise he's a total and utter plonker. His fave singer is J. Lo, for chrissake. And he screams out his own name during love making.

How do you let him down gently? You don't want to be too blunt on account of he's the sensitive type (remember that yarn he told you about being bullied in kindergarten?) but you'd prefer to have lighted matches placed under your fingernails than to spend another evening listening to him wittering on about how you've turned his life around and he wants lots of babies with you 'or die trying'.

The following suggestions may prove useful to get out of a pickle if he won't take no for answer, or you simply can't bring yourself to tell him.

(1) Change your phone number.

(2) Tell him he's a 'sweet guy' but you're 'not ready for a relationship just yet' because you've got a lot of 'stuff' to get your head around and the idea of 'sharing space' with someone at the minute will have to stay on the 'back burner'. (OK, it sounds like you got it out of an American soap, but he'll believe it because his ego won't accept that you'd rather date Dracula.)

40

(3) Go into one of those theatrical shops and buy a wig, glasses and false eyelashes. The Groucho Marx tache is optional. If this doesn't work, how about radical plastic surgery?

(4) Make up a story about having a major promotion at work which entails two years in Colombia, emphasising that he'll be the first person you look up when you get back. Yeah, right. If he suggests writing point out the dire straits that the Colombian postal services are in to deter him.

(5) Tell him your canary died and you have to go to the funeral. It's a very special canary.

If that little lot doesn't work and he's still clogging up your phone line with special pleading (he managed to beat suggestion 1, the persistent little shit) and arriving at your doorstep at all hours of the day and night with daffs and love poems, try these slightly more extreme stratagems.

(1) Tell him you're pregnant with triplets.

(2) Your mother's stepcousin from Bradford is a manic depressive and the whole family are moving 'to be there for her'. Aren't these American soaps great?

(3) You yourself are a paranoid schizophrenic with quasi-messianic notions of world domination. You're also suicidal and believe you were kidnapped by aliens and injected with a serum that means you definitely won't live beyond the age of twenty-three. Or if you do, you'll develop a third breast.

(4) This condition is contagious if you're touched.

Chapter 2
Request

There's nothing more expensive than a girl who's free for the evening.

(Hal Roach)

The first date

I'm not your type, my breasts are real.

(Janeane Garofalo)

Going on a first date with a girl is a serious financial investment if not a downright gamble. Not only could the price of buying her a drink pay off the debt of a small South American republic; she may well seduce you with a wiggle of her hips and a coy smile, making you feel that you're actually enjoying putting a considerable dent in your wallet.

As well as providing all the liquid refreshment, you may have to listen to her talk like a Gatling gun. She'll have to speak up if you're going to be able to hear her over the music in the super-trendy new bar she's suggested you take her to, despite the fact you wouldn't be seen dead in there by your mates. Something in the deeper recesses of your psyche might feel like saying 'You could have a nice personality. Why do you spoil it by opening your mouth?' Of course this would torpedo your chances of achieving the big score.

Respite is at hand however when she stops talking and pointedly plays with her twizzle stick, chasing the ice around the empty glass and not saying a word until you've bought her another. Now you must make an executive decision. Either (A): buy her another drink and confirm that this is a date and commit yourself to her for the rest of the evening in the hope of a BIG payoff at the end of the night or (B): Run.

If you chose option (A): Dig deep into your beleaguered pocket for your last remaining pennies and if you can pluck up enough courage ask her if she's ever thought of going Dutch. 'You want me to go to Amsterdam with you?' she'll smile sweetly, her face full of innocence.

However, don't despair, this is the easy part. After a few drinks, you have to gauge the right moment to put your arm around her. Lighten the mood, tell her a few jokes. Even if you're as funny as a heart attack, she'll find it too embarrassing not to laugh and by this time you'll have had a few and won't care. Plus you can get your own back for her talking at you during the initial stages of the date.

One way to estimate the right time is by letting her make the first move. This won't be a big one and may well be totally invisible to the untrained eye. She may play with her hair (lukewarm encouragement) or even touch her neck and giggle nervously at your jokes (a better sign). If she laughs heartily and briefly touches your knee that's a green light for some cuddling. Lean towards her and put your arm around her shoulders. It'll really hurt after a while but it's the only way to progress on to the next step: the kiss. The longer you cuddle her the less likely she is to

---

Men are those creatures with two legs
and eight hands.
(Jayne Mansfield)

---

slap you. After a little time with your arm around her waist buy her another drink. At this point you'll find your heart racing, your mind working fifteen to the dozen and your being infused with a complete inability to get any drunker as adrenalin courses through your body.

As the lubrication begins to work she'll feel like dancing and drag you out onto the floor. The dance floor is a place for two things.

(1) Ideal for the first kiss to that slow song. Cheesy and yet irresistibly cute to the female mind.

(2) A place for making a complete prat out of yourself because of your utter inability to comprehend rhythm, control your bodily movements or look remotely human.

Try to put off this moment as long as possible which will increase your opportunity of getting a snog and decrease the chances that she'll notice you dancing like a spider on acid. After that it's all a question of waiting for the right song. Then it's kisses and gropes the rest of the way.

As the music winds down for the night it's time to broach the question, 'Your place or mine?' However, a little tact can go a long way. 'Want to share a taxi?' is a far more gentlemanly overture, implying that more is available if she wants it and not essential if she doesn't. Of course she's highly unlikely to be in a state to do anything physical so you'll have to share the taxi anyway because it's just not on to abandon your inebriated date in a gutter in Leicester Square. When she falls asleep hiccuping with her head on your shoulder you can rest assured that sex is probably out of the question, unless she gets a second wind or you've remembered to get that extra-strength, full-caffeine, full-fat, extra-sugar coffee in. At least you'll have to take her back to your place and get to wake up in bed with her. On such nights are many relationships built.

I once went out with a guy who asked me to mother him,
so I spat on a hankie and wiped his face.
(Jenny Jones)

Subjects to be avoided

Religion, politics and death go without saying but there are more dangers in the conversation minefield than you would imagine. Yes, I'm talking about the 'F' word: Feminism. The vast majority of girls claim they aren't feminists. Bra-burning is so passé and fanatical. At heart all women are absolutely convinced of their own superiority over men, but with a few simple steps you can avoid any possible antagonism.

Never ever refer to women as ladies. Invariably they prefer 'women' and while you think you're being complimentary you may find yourself suddenly faced with your female companion jumping out of her chair and shouting: 'Stop using sexist terms like that!' By which time it's too late and you'll be sucked into an argument during which you'll have to say something along the lines of: 'My problem is not with what they were fighting for in a social, careerist and political context but how they achieved such aims.' This is of course a perfectly reasonable point of view. Unless you're a woman.

You'll now be faced with a full-on wobbly, at which point you'll be thinking and perhaps saying something as foolish as: 'This is why it's so difficult to get on with people like …' You won't be allowed to finish your Last Will and Testament before she says: 'You're one of those chauvinists who think we all have to be submissive and docile and then you'll grant us the honour of actually liking us!' You can of course substitute the word chauvinist for a variety of five and indeed six or seven lettered words beginning with s, f or b.

You may try to retaliate, 'No, you've misunderstood me. What I meant was that in my humble view feminism has done more to create a divisiveness between the sexes than emceepeeism. And now we have all those emasculated, de-sexualised males running around the place looking for their gonads or testosterone or what have you. This leaves you women complaining that all their male friends are such wimps.' Of course before you can deliver the first three words of this rather masterly example of oratory and debate you'll find yourself in a growing space of emptiness as your date digs her index finger into your jugular vein. If you survive you may reflect on the words of Norman Mailer, that well-known chauvinist who said that he used to love and idolise women before feminism reared its head. 'It was only then,' he said 'that I realised women could be as mean and selfish and stubborn and aggressive and petty as men.' Having reflected on the social-cultural implications of this deep philosophical point, you can start hitting the beers. Alone again, naturally.

First date blues

Brains are never a handicap to a girl if she hides them under a see-through blouse.

(Bobby Vinton)

Waiting for him to make the first move can be tortuous enough. But now he's done it the pain is really going to begin. Gone are the days where a would-be Sir Galahad would arrange a date, via your parents, and arrive all brushed up with a bunch of daffodils. Long vanished are the bourgeois niceties and the pillow talks and the walking into doors as you fantasise about what he's really like. Instead we have strategising, plotting and second-guessing.

The venue of that stress-inducing first date is a major bone of contention. Do you go out to a ritzy restaurant and spend the evening engaged in artificial chatter, or suggest sitting in with a pizza and a video?

And then there's the vexed question of who pays? If you did the asking, is it your responsibility? Or will this make the man in question unnerved? What if he's out of work

---

A woman talks to one man, looks at a second and thinks of a third.
(Milton Berle)

---

and you aren't? Does romance go out the window if you go Dutch? 'If I'm dating a guy who can afford to take me out to dinner,' said one woman, 'I have no qualms about

> *Women are like banks. breaking*
> *and entering is a serious business.*
> (Joe Orton)

spending his money. If he can barely make ends meet, I'll split it. But there are just some things in life that men do and some that women do. I'm sorry, but that's the way it is. We have to carry the baby and menstruate every month. If they can afford it, they can pay for the goddam meal!'

Now that the finances are sorted out, the next major issue is: who plants the first kiss? And, if and when it happens, how should you react? One woman's attitude was: 'You're supposed to act like you're overcome by the moment he makes his move to kiss you, as if it's the first time the thought of sex has entered your head – but you've really been thinking about it all night, and so has he.'

But, this being the twenty-first century, what happens if he's too slow or too shy and you decide you can't wait any longer and start the canoodling yourself? One embarrassed man confessed that the only time a woman had kissed him first, he reeled back in horror. It wasn't that he didn't want a kiss, he said, or even that he objected to her executing it – it was just a surprising new experience, and it threw him.

The main problematical area at a date's end is whether a man should say 'I'll call you' (the coward's way out), or if you should reply 'That would be wonderful' even if you've decided he's a complete wanker. It's probably easier if both of you are lying at the same time; if one cares and the other doesn't it can be hurtful. It's one of the worst experiences if he leaves you hanging by the phone while he's tottled off to some other woman for a quickie.

The good news about the twenty-first century girl is the flirting. Because of the nineties, men are absolutely terrified of doing anything in case they get landed with a sexual harassment suit. You, on the other hand, have no such worries. As the behavioural scientists discovered: 'While men appear to be sexual aggressors, they are in fact responding to subtle signals that women, the cleverer darlings, are sending out. Women draw men to them with the glint of an eye, seductive posture, tone of voice, pressure of touch – all those gestures referred to as "display" in the animal kingdom.'

Maybe the bottom line is nothing has really changed. We all have to go out there into the concrete jungle of emotions and slug it out, for better or for worse, before two mismatches self-destruct.

Filling in time between dates

Dating's like childbirth. You forget how awful it is until the next time.

(Anon.)

(1) Go shopping for that new pair of shoes you need, and at least four other pairs you don't.

(2) Sit by the phone waiting for him to tell you how great the last date was and inviting you on another.

(3) Take the initiative and stalk him until he gets the message and invites you on another date

(4) Dye your hair purple with orange highlights, just to surprise him when next he sees you.

(5) Decide that he's too slow and go in search of another nice young man to take you out and lavish time, money and attention on you.

Love is just a three letter word

If sex is such a natural phenomenon, how come there are
so many books on how to do it?
(Bette Midler)

Sex.

I decided to place the word in a paragraph of its own just to get your attention. Not that I needed to. Put the word anywhere and you've got everyone agog. 'Sex has been a part of my life for as long as I can remember', said Gyles Brandreth, 'In fact on the day of my birth you would have found me in bed with an older woman.'

Once upon a time the air was clean and the sex was dirty. In those days when a grope in the back seat of a cinema on Saturday night was generally geared to earn you the wrath of the padres the next time you went to confession. Alas, all that has changed, changed utterly. A terrible sexuality is born.

What comes first in a relationship
is lust, then more lust.
(Jacqueline Bisset)

These days chastity is only one of the sexual perversions we really recognise – a disease, that, if spotted early, can possibly be cured.

Self-styled boudoir psychologist Wendy Dennis puts it well: 'Thanks to the women's movement, female orgasms now come in deluxe models and neon-bright hues, and one has only to switch on Oprah Winfrey to get a fast breaking news update on orgasm quality control.'

In the old days women were terrified of unprotected sex because of the fear of pregnancy, and all that implied. Today the goalposts have shifted with the pill, changing mores, and a plethora of single mums being embraced into society without the Scarlet Woman tag hanging over them. But unsafe sex still carries the terror of AIDS.

In fact the main problem assailing people today isn't whether or not to take precautions but who exactly should take the initiative. If a woman brings a condom on a date she's afraid she'll be called fast. If a man does, he might be deemed presumptuous – or lacking respect. To alleviate the problem, one woman suggests that people should keep a bowl of condoms on their coffee table and have done with it. 'You bring the condoms' another modern woman advocated to her date 'and I'll bring the wine.' Alas, whatever happened to the smoochy Sinatra numbers in the background and the agonising build-up to that first kiss?

Sex got me into trouble from the age of fifteen.
I'm hoping that by the time I'm seventy
I'll straighten out.
(Harold Robbins)

Sometimes I wonder if we've thrown the baby out with the bath-water. As Ms Dennis puts it, sex on the first date may well turn out to be sex on the last date. And the pyrotechnics of will-I-won't-I has acquired almost farci-cal ramifications. The rationalisations go like this, says Wendy: 'She's got nicely manicured nails – she's safe. He's got custom made suits – he's okay.' One woman she talked to got out her AIDS pocket calculator and did the mathematics: 'Let's see. This guy says he's been 15 years in a monogamous marriage and he tells me he hardly slept around in his single days. I'll pass.'

In America today, having an AIDS test prior to going on a date is almost as routine as working out – or attempting a low-fat diet. To this extent, those who've been good boys and girls during the '90s are very desirable lovers for

Lead me not into temptation. I can find the way myself.
(Rita Mae Brown)

those terrified of becoming HIV positive – and who isn't. As one erstwhile abstemious woman put it to her would-be Romeo: 'The good news is, I'm low risk. The bad news is I'm probably rusty.'

Sex isn't always a problem in relationships. A decade ago a fashion swept through the US where over 500,000 teenagers signed a pledge to remain 'pure' until marriage. The movement was started back in 1992 by a Southern Minister in a campaign called True Love Waits. 100,000 teenagers descended upon Orlando in Florida for a convention and more than 500,000 attended in Washington, staking their 'True Love Waits' placards on Capitol Hill.

Teenagers took vows of chastity before their parents, who were probably at it all the time at their age in the '60s and '70s during the post-war and post-Woodstock baby-boom. They wore T-shirts saying 'I'm a virgin and proud of it.' Some were even wearing gold rings as a sign of the no-sex pact, which would only be taken off and given to their spouse on the wedding night. No doubt the fad reduced the number of young single mothers. No doubt it also reduced STDs. One thing it surely did was persuade the entire male youth population to get married at their earliest convenience, raising a whole host of other problems, not to mention divorce, later in the relationship. Ah well – only in America, as the saying goes.

Ten things a man says to a woman before sex

(1) Your hair looks gorgeous.
(2) We really should spend more time together.
(3) You're far too good for me.
(4) Here's a little prezzie.
(5) Why don't you turn the lights down?
(6) Every minute away from you is like an hour.
(7) I'm going to splurge out on our summer holiday this year.
(8) You get more beautiful every day.
(9) I don't think I've ever been happier.
(10) You ARE on the, you know, aren't you?

Ten things a man says to a woman during sex

(1) Uuuuungh
(2) Pshawt
(3) Grwnp
(4) Pghytiuop
(5) Nylummri
(6) Fgtuuilkj
(7) Swooftghyl
(8) Cghlkssswop
(9) Cwnnopq
(10) Whew, that was great, wasn't it? Darling, why are you crying?

Ten things a man says after sex

(1)
(2)
(3)
(4)
(5)
(6)
(7)
(8)
(9)
(10) ZZZZZzzzzzzzzzzz

Definition of terms

When I delivered my son Ramon I was so stupid I thought the placenta was his twin.

(Martin Sheen)

The world of sex can be a dangerous place for the uninitiated. So before you accidentally commit yourself to some BDSM or sangvamp at the local Torture Garden you may wish to consult this dictionary to acquaint yourself with the lingo.

Adolescence: The stage between infancy and adultery.

Anatomy: Something everyone has, but it looks better on a woman.

Bisexual: Someone who likes women as much as the next man.

Bigamy: Making the same mistake twice.

Bra: Booby trap.

Career girl: A woman who's made it to the top because her dresses didn't.

Celibacy: Not an inherited characteristic.

Circumcision: A bloody rip-off.

Courtship: The period of a girl's life where she decides if she can do any better.

Condominium: A prophylactic for midgets.

Coq au vin: Sex in a lorry.

Eunuch: A man who has his work cut out for him.

Flattery: Telling your boyfriend exactly what he thinks of himself.

Frustration: The first time you realise she won't let you do it a second time.

Desperation: The second time you realise she won't let you do it again.

Flirt: A girl who thinks it's every man for herself.

Funeral: A wedding with one less drunk.

Gigolo: Fee-male.

Incest: A relatively boring activity.

Irish Romance: 5 minutes of sex, and 55 years of guilt.

Lingerie: What brings out the breast in a woman and the beast in a man.

Mother's Day: What happens nine months after father's night.

Necrophilia: A dead boring activity.

Orgy: Group therapy.

Oral sex: A matter of taste.

Possibly: No way!

Puberty: A hair-raising experience.

Punctuality: The art of guessing how late your date is going to be.

Sado-masochism: Never having to say you're sorry.

Seduction: The art of genital persuasion.

Strip Poker: A game where, the more you lose, the more you have to show for it.

Successful husband: A man who earns more than his wife can spend.

Transvestite: Someone who wants to eat, drink and be Mary.

Virgin: Frozen asset.

Wedding: A funeral where you can smell your own flowers.

Youthful figure: What you get when you ask a woman her age.

Words from the wise

It's the fallen women who are usually picked up.
(Woody Allen)

William Faulkner felt that one of the saddest things about life was that the only thing you could do for eight hours at a go was work. 'You can't eat, or drink, or make love for eight hours', he noted.

Racing maestro Stirling Moss believed there were two things a man would never admit he couldn't do well: drive and make love. Robert Helpman said that the trouble with nude dancing was that not everything stopped when the music did.

'If it weren't for pickpockets,' said Rodney Dangerfield, 'I'd have no sex life at all.' Andy Warhol had a typically

quirky attitude to the whole subject: 'Love and sex can go together' he said 'and sex and unlove can go together, and love and unsex. But personal love and personal sex is bad.' I haven't the faintest idea what he's talking about but it sounds good and proves that geniuses do live in quite different places to the rest of us.

A woman should be obscene and not heard.
(John Lennon)

Alan O'Brien confessed to having done 'almost every activity inside a taxi that doesn't require mains drainage' – which must have given the cabbie a good reason to peek through the rear view mirror when waiting for the lights to go green.

Woody Allen believes sex is only dirty if it's done right, unlike Madonna who feels it's only dirty if you don't have a bath first. Woody did concede however that while sex wasn't the answer it raised some pretty good questions. Arnold Bax thought we should all make a point of trying every experience once – 'except incest and folk dancing.'

Of course we all know that males are predators and out for the One Thing. Who can forget the classic bit of graffiti: For a man sex is like a bank, when you withdraw you lose interest. Phallic thimble Dudley Moore once said he was looking for a meaningful one-night stand. It's hard to know if he was joking or not.

Maybe the most profound sexologist of our times is the aforementioned Mr Allen, try as he might to trivialise his insights. Woody is the man who once told us that sex without love is an empty experience … but as empty experiences go it's one of the best.

A pun may be the lowest form of wit, but many a true

word is said in jest. Woody extracted the michael from a whole generation of trick-cycling sex experts when he moaned 'I've finally had an orgasm after all these years – and my doctor tells me it's the wrong kind.' Well someone had to say it. In fact it's difficult to pick up a woman's magazine or book today without somebody telling us what we should be doing to who, and how often, so we can get the Big 'O' right.

Jackie Onassis said sex was a bad thing because it rumpled her bedclothes. Quentin Crisp called it the last refuge of the miserable. For Clifford Odets it was the poor man's polo. Charles Bukowski was somewhat more colourful. He likened it to 'kissing death in the arse while singing'. These people were definitely not doing it right.

We like to think we're enlightened about it these days. Of course people still blush at stag parties, phallic jokes, kiss-o-grams, contentious Hollywood scenes, naughty limericks, holiday postcards and double entendres (not to mention books ... Ed.). Perhaps they always will. And perhaps the more wars we fight about freedom of expression, the more we're protesting about, or admitting, our innate inhibitions.

The big difference between sex for money and sex for free is that sex for money costs less.
(Brendan Francis)

Go to any bar any night of the week and sex is the subject that gets the most nudges and winks. Macho may not be mucho but it's still guaranteed to get the best feedback for money in the company of leering males. You have to ask yourself the question: Would we be nostalgic if wolf-whistles went the way of all flesh? Or if Kilroy, God forbid, finally came out of the closet and identified him(her?)self with something more than a squiggle of bluish eye line?

Half the fun of sex is the guilt and remorse.

All this fuss over sex and we have to ask: Is it over-rated? Evelyn Waugh said he'd prefer to go to the dentist for physical pleasure. He sounds like a really big ball of laughs. Henry Miller went to the other extreme. He said it was one of the nine reasons for reincarnation … and the other eight didn't matter. It took Mort Sahl to reach a compromise: 'Sex is about as important as a cheese sandwich. But if you ain't got one to put in your belly, a cheese sandwich can be very important.'

Of course if you're without your sandwich you can always resort to more desperate measures. In the 1960s we heard a lot about 'free love' but things have changed in the interim … just ask Hugh Grant.

Police investigating the books of New York's most expensive madam in 1984 came across an account of a Saudi prince who spent £100,000 on a single night out. He hired thirty £1,000-a-night girls from a high-class agency and took them along with nine friends and relatives to ten £1,500-a-day suites at the top of the Waldorf Tower Hotel. First they feasted on a £30,000 meal and then prepared for bed with their chosen partners after firing corks from dozens of Dom Perignon bottles at each other.

If you haven't got £100,000 to burn you could always improvise. A couple in Portsmouth were so skint they didn't even have the train fare so they came up with a brilliant idea. They nipped into a photo-booth and took some pornographic pictures of themselves and flogged them. At this juncture we should point out that they had only met each other 15 minutes before. They made a tidy sum.

A good scam was thought up in Sweden by a man who requested a tax rebate in the Swedish high court on the basis that he had to pay prostitutes to alleviate 'abnormally severe depression'. Unfortunately the judge didn't buy it.

Another cautionary tale involved one Al Hamburg who, in 1984, sold his car to a girl for sex sessions. To make the deal official he handed her a special chart with fifty stick-on gold stars to keep record of how they were doing. Thirty-three sessions into the bargain – some in bed, some in the car – she said she was too exhausted to continue. She drove away in the car and refused to come back. Al took her to court for breach of contract but the magistrate ruled in favour of the girl. After all, thirty-three is well over half-way towards fifty.

The law can be a tricky thing when it comes to sex. In 1981, crowds of shoppers in a Montevideo market stared in astonishment as a middle-aged couple lay down behind the stalls and had sex in the gutter. A court later dismissed the charge of indecency on the grounds that their doctor had told them to introduce as much variety as possible to their lovemaking.

But if having sex in different places doesn't work you can always take the route of Louis Pilar of Rheims. When police charged him with shooting and wounding his wife he blamed a 3-week TV strike, saying 'There was nothing to look at. I was bored.' If you think that's a surprising plea, bear in mind that his wife supported it. 'I don't blame him' she remembered, 'It's really been boring in the evenings.'

Other problems can occur when couples are too close. In 1963 a massive traffic jam resulted in Rio de Janeiro due to an apparently passionate teenage pair locked in an inter-minable embrace. For two and a half hours they remained static as the traffic lights changed and the car horns honked. Police were called but it was a dentist who finally solved the problem: he disentangled their dental braces.

Sometimes legal decisions can be affected by the prudery of those in charge. Some years ago when a judge heard a plaintiff complaining that his sex life was destroyed by an accident with a bulldozer, he asked if he was married. When counsel replied that he wasn't, the judge threw the case out of court.

And then there was the case of the flat-chested bank cashier who decided to use some of the money she was handling to supplement her not too vital statistics and impress her boyfriend. When she was accused of stealing, her argument was, 'I meant to bring back the money but my date went so badly I forgot.' Which just goes to show that men aren't only interested in big breasts.

Neither are juries above reproach. There was a case in Santa Cruz where a judge dismissed one of his jurors, saying: 'This woman is my wife. She never pays any attention to what I say at home and I have no reason to believe her behaviour in court would be any different.' Doesn't your heart go right out to him?

Just because most judges are male, don't come under the misapprehension that the law favours men. In the town of Pixie, Idaho, if a woman berates her husband in public and a crowd gathers, the husband can be fined. In Iowa the situation is worse for married and unmarried men: a man can be arrested for winking at a woman he doesn't know.

What every girl should know is: better.
(Anon.)

But the law doesn't always penalise the over-sexed. There was the case of the couple who booked into a Vancouver hotel for $78. When the service waiter came into the room the next morning with the couple's break-fast he found four other couples there and a ten-person orgy in full swing. When the hotel manager added an extra $300 to the man's bill he refused to pay, saying he'd booked a family room for the original price. Since the hotel hadn't stipulated how many people could occupy a family room, the court ruled in favour of the randy couple.

Another case that was thrown out of court involved a wife who had been proved to have thrown almost every domestic utensil at her husband. The reason? She had missed him on almost every occasion and thereby wasn't deemed to have been guilty of cruelty.

The judge in a rape case found himself confronted with an even dodgier issue. The woman claiming to have been raped had removed her petticoat in the accused's car on the night of the incident and this was giving the judge some pause. Her argument? 'It was rather an expensive one, you see. I knew what he was going to do but I was so frightened I couldn't stop him. I asked him if I could take it off because I didn't want it to get crumpled.' There's nothing like a cool head under pressure.

Barbie is getting a bigger waist and a smaller chest.
Not surprisingly, Ken announced he wants to
start seeing other dolls.
(David Letterman)

It's not only humans whose sex lives end up in court either. It happens to animals as well. A Sicilian pet-owner was once fined after his dog had been found guilty of 'committing an obscene act in a public place'. Which is similar to the case of a man who was granted a divorce from his wife after the latter insisted that he kiss her, her sister and the cat after coming home from work every day. You just never know what oddities you're committing yourself to in marriage.

Sometimes one feels like putting the authorities in the dock. I doubt that the gay community was impressed with the psychologist in Luton some years ago speaking on behalf of a sixteen-year-old boy accused of molesting two girls. This is what the judge was heard to say: 'Previously he's been found guilty of offences which suggested a homosexual nature. The latest offences are at least a step in the right direction.' And who says that the justice system is in dire need of modernising?

Often it's hard to know if you even *want* to be convicted or not. In 1985 in Ohio a judge dismissed an indecency charge brought against a stripper because her act failed to arouse the arresting vice squad detective. You can't help thinking the case musn't have done much good for her attendance figures afterwards.

I have bursts of being a lady, but it
doesn't last long.
(Shelly Winters)

An exotic dancer called Mavisa Lopez, in a similar case, fared differently. She was asked for a courtroom demonstration of her act, and when she was finished the jury was so impressed it broke into spontaneous applause. The bad news is that Mavisa had an indecency fine promptly slapped on her. You win some, you lose some.

Truly, madly, deeply

Husband: 'If I was poor would you still love me?'
Wife: 'Yes, but I'd miss you terribly.'

Model Anna Nicole Smith was awarded £325 million by a court because she married a very rich man in his eighties and he died shortly afterwards. His children are livid, understandably, but Anna Nicole insists she 'loved, loved, loved' the old man dearly.

Oil tycoon Howard Marshall was eighty-nine when she married him. He died fourteen months after they walked up the aisle together in 1994. His family, says former *Playboy* model Nicole, 'didn't understand the age thing. They didn't understand the love thing.' Really?

'He took me out of a terrible place,' said the former drug and booze addict, 'He was a saviour.' I'll say he was! Nicole now says she talks to a picture of Howard she keeps on her wall, but refuses to reveal what she says. I've got a good guess: Thank you, thank you, thank you.

Nicole says she rebuffed Howard's marriage proposals for two years for fear of being called a gold-digger. Nicole – we'd never think that! When she did her erotic dancing, she says, Howard got all excited and grabbed her breasts. Not bad for an eighty-nine-year-old. But was it worth £325 million?

How is it that you never see models falling in love with old men who are poor? Or, for that matter, poor old men falling in love with women who aren't models? Did you ever hear of a man trading in his wife for an older model? Julie Birchill has an interesting take on the subject. 'Rule One,' she says 'is that the sun will never rise in the west.' Rule Two is even better: 'As long as there are rich men trying not to feel old, there will be young girls trying not to feel poor.'

Help for the broken-hearted

A terrible thing happened to me last night – nothing.
(Phyllis Diller)

You went out, had a good time, you were funny, articulate and danced well, you drank and whiled away the hours … and ended up asleep alone in your own bed and now he won't return your calls. He didn't even want a one night stand. What's wrong with you?

Author Cathy Hopkins' advice in her book *What To Do After the Kissing Stops* is both varied and versatile. Her first suggestion to take your mind off a wandering and/or love-less male is to throw all your attention into food. Why? Because you'll never see a piece of steak backing off your plate saying 'Oh no, not you, you've got bad breath.' Or 'I saw you in that Thai place last night and you think you can come here and start where you left off.' Plus when you've had enough of said repast you don't have to make any excuses for leaving.

Another alternative, she suggests, is jogging – though she's not too keen on it herself. 'In the long run, exercise isn't a bad idea – but a short run is enough for most of us.' In addition to which she feels most joggers are miserable creatures. ' I think they run to punish themselves for some deep dark, guilty secret. A bit of self-torture makes up for the dead body in the cellar.'

If you're tempted to deal with the pain by having therapy, however, resist it. They'll only say things like 'Your elder brother tried to kill you when he was two and a half and you haven't felt safe since.' Or 'You had a bad birth experience and you keep recreating what's familiar.'

A first cousin of therapy is the dreaded weekend workshop. If you opt for this, make sure you prepare yourself for the following familiar workshopspeak. 'I've discovered my female side' means 'I cry at sad movies'. 'I've discovered my male side' means 'I got drunk, punched someone, fell asleep in a gutter and woke up in a police cell'. 'I'm on a learning curve' means 'I don't have a bloody clue what I'm doing'. 'It was a valuable lesson' means 'I totally cocked up.'

Less hardcore masochists may try philosophy and ask all those soulsearching questions, getting to the real you. 'Why are we here?' 'Where did we come from?' Or, on a more practical level: 'What do you give a sick florist?' 'Where do all those lost socks go?' And the even more fundamental: 'How do people who drive snowploughs get to work?' Unfortunately any answers you find won't necessarily relate to why that bastard won't talk to you anymore.

The only solution to this problem is to pick yourself up, dust yourself off and get back into the game. Either that or take up magic and specialise in the sawing-men-in-half trick to work out your anger.

The final word

Did you hear about the woman who stabbed her husband thirty-seven times? I admire her restraint.

(Roseanne)

Not every relationship you have will work out, for a variety of reasons.

If you find that your partner has been cheating on you, you could follow the example of Peter the Great. Upon discovering that his wife had been unfaithful he had her lover executed and then decapitated, which was par for the course in those days. But he added a nice touch: he had the head preserved in an alcohol-filled jar and placed in the Queen's boudoir as a reminder of her misdemeanour. Perhaps today this wouldn't be such an acceptable way of communicating your feelings of betrayal and outrage, but it has style.

If you want a less drastic method of saying goodbye then you can purchase a bunch of dead flowers from an American called Michael Mirsch. He'll deliver a dozen carefully picked but wilted roses bound with a black silk ribbon to tell your estranged lover that Cupid isn't firing his arrows into your heart anymore.

If this doesn't get the message across, a way to really end the relationship with a girl with total finality is very simple. Sleep with her mother and/or sister. It's a guaranteed passage, first class, back to singledom and you'll never have to see her again. However, you might want to be wary of signing up to any message boards on the net like Friends Reunited where one outraged woman put the major points of her man's misdemeanour in graphic detail, as well as his current address and phone number for all to see.

Chapter 3
Conquest

It is a woman's business to get married
as soon as possible; and a man's to keep unmarried
as long as he can.

(George Bernard Shaw)

The honourable institution

Marriage is neither heaven nor hell – it is simply purgatory.

(Abraham Lincoln)

George Bernard Shaw said marriage was popular because it combined the maximum of temptation with the maximum of opportunity. In many ways, perhaps the opposite of this is true. It's hard to read an agony column in a tabloid newspaper these days without hearing about at least one marriage that's on the rocks because the two people are bored with each other – at least from a sexual angle. Does familiarity breed? Or is it likelier to breed contempt?

Zsa Zsa Gabor said you never really know a man until you divorce him – and she should be an authority on the subject. The Russian author Pushkin said 'The less we love a woman, the more we are loved by her.' Does the same reverse psychology apply to men? Or more so to them? Marilyn Monroe believed that, yes, husbands did make good lovers … but mostly when they were in bed with women who weren't their wives. You might ask how she knew this.

A bride got so nervous on her wedding day that she accidentally said 'I did'.
(Roy Brown)

Most thinking people tend to rail against the sacrament of matrimony, even – or especially – if they've been

73

involved in it for a long time themselves. If it's as bad as the average wag, or graffiti merchant, makes out, how come it's still in existence? Presumably some people are getting something out of it. Are we allowed to be boring and say that, like everything else, you get out of it what you put into it? People who expect the world to move usually end up moving themselves to the marriage counsellor. Or worse again, the divorce courts.

Gags about gay (and I don't mean *that* type of gay) bachelors and near-suicidal henpecked husbands – or cockpecked wives – are almost as much an institution as the one they exult in denigrating. Viz. ... 'Home Sweet Home must surely have been written by a bachelor': 'I'm not going to make the same mistake once': 'Why buy a cow when you can get the milk for free?': 'Bachelors know more about women than married men – if they didn't they'd be married too.' Et cetera, ad nauseam.

Hollywood actor Henry Fonda was somewhat more light-hearted when he commented way back in 1968: 'My son got his first film role, playing a man who's been married for thirty years. I told him to stick at it and next time he might get a speaking part.'

I never knew what real happiness was until I got married and by then it was too late.
(Max Kaufmann)

The poet Samuel Taylor Coleridge noted 'The most happy marriage I can picture would be the union of a deaf man to a blind woman'. To be fair to him, he was kinder than Fonda, admitting as he did that there are as many ugly men as voluble women. Not that either stereotype exists in large numbers, but why should truth get in the way of a good line?

Prospective son-in-law: I've come to ask for your daughter's hand in marriage.
Father: Why not, you've had everything else.

Another reason for the reluctance of people to marry is the frightening divorce rate. And, if you're rich, the attendant alimony. 'The screwing you get for the screwing you got' as one wit put it. Actor Jack Nicholson said recently that this was the greatest deterrent to marriage for himself, if not his bachelor cronies. I'm sure people like Sly Stallone and Johnny Carson would agree – not to mention the bold Donald Trump. Mick Jagger observed that marriage was like signing a 356-page contract without knowing what's in it, but again he's an individual who's been known to get some satisfaction out of it. Alan Jay Lerner said he was a great fan of the opposite sex, 'and I have the bills to prove it'. Somehow I feel his ex's lawyer might have had something to do with his magnanimity in this regard.

Maybe the most negative comment ever made about marriage was that of the German thinker Arthur Schopenhauer. He said 'Most men fall in love with a pretty face, but find themselves bound for life to a hateful stranger, alternating endlessly between a workshop and a witch's kitchen.'

Along the same tack, there's a Mexican proverb, which goes, 'Marriage is the only war where one sleeps with the enemy'. Which again raises the question … why? I mean are people naturally that masochistic?

The A-Z of weddings

I spent so much on my girlfriend I decided to marry her for my money.

(Richard Pryor)

A is for ALCOHOL, which you'll be having lots of at yours, chiefly to make you see double and feel single.

B is for BLOTTO, which you get if you've had enough A.

C is for CHILDREN, which women sometimes produce after getting B with A.

D is for DRIVING, which you're not to do when B if you want to be alive for H (see H).

E is for ERRATIC, which is the way you D when B.

F is for a four lettered word which I'm far to polite to utter here.

G is for GIFTS, most of which will be about as much use to you as an ashtray on a motorbike.

H is for HONEYMOON, the time of your life when you realise that the person you M (see M) wasn't at all like you thought she was.

I is for IN-LAWS … who will soon become your outlaws.

J is for JOINED. Which you now are to your spouse: the two as one. Just make sure you're the one.

K is for KISSING, which you'll be doing a lot of during the next few days – hopefully to your betrothed.

L is for LOVE, a much more dangerous word than F.

M is for MARRIED, which you now are RIP.

N is for NIAGRA FALLS, the second biggest disappointment of the average H.

O is the figure in your bank account after you've paid for R (see R).

P is PARENTS who are people who practice V (see V).

Q is for QUEER which is a decidedly unPC term for homosexuals, unless you're from Ireland where it is a term for a man who prefers women to Guinness.

R is for RECEPTION which is where you get B because you've just realised you're M.

S is for STAG PARTY at which you tried to seduce the stripogram girl before you realised it was Uncle Fred in disguise.

T is for TROUBLE which follows M because your new wife has suddenly found out what happened at S when you had partaken of too much A and gotten B.

U is for UNTAMEABLE which you used to be before your wife turned you from an old rake into a lawn mower.

V is for VATICAN ROULETTE aka the rhythm method of birth control which Catholics are now allowed to do as part of a loving relationship.

W is for WORK which is what you have just signed up for the next forty years to prevent O.

X is for all those kisses people will plant on you lips, cheeks and other (unmentionable) parts at the R under the influence of A.

Y is for YOUTH, which is a disease from which you are now officially cured after M.

ZZZZ is what your wife does when you come back B from the H instead of giving you L.

Marriage is very difficult. Very few of us are fortunate enough to marry multi-millionaire girls with 39-inch busts who have undergone frontal lobotomies.
(Tony Curtis)

Wedding belles

The first part of our marriage was wonderful. But then on the way back from the ceremony ...

(Henny Youngman)

It's never too late to change your mind. No matter how well you feel you know your partner, it does no harm to have a last Major Think about his suitability and sincerity before you walk up the aisle. Marriage may be a lottery, but you can't tear up your ticket if you lose. It's probably safe to say your Significant Other may not be marrying you for the right reasons if he:

(1) Loses the ring.

(2) Doesn't get to the church on time.

(3) Doesn't get to the church at all.

(4) Sleeps with one of the bridesmaids the night before the wedding.

(5) Get so drunk that he forgets your name at the ceremony.

(6) Insists on mooning before your parents at the reception.

(7) Tells you he's gay.

(8) Wants to bring the best man on the honeymoon.

(9) Tells you he wants to watch you have sex with the best man.

(10) Is actually a woman.

Some of these revelations are obviously coming at a bad time. If you've been going out with 'him' for four years, it may be something of shock to discover that 'he' has a vagina instead of a penis, but then they always say take him for at least one test-drive before you buy. It's something a lot of potential brides forget to ask before the Big Day, probably because of all the things they have to think about, like who sits next to who at the reception, whether Uncle Alfred will cause a ruckus after he has his third G & T, and who's going to feed the hamsters while you're on your honeymoon.

If he's male but homosexual, maybe this isn't as bad as it sounds. Try to look on the bright side, at least he's got all the right bits. Maybe he's heterosexual but in denial. If so, better latent than never.

The idea of wanting to bring the best man on the honeymoon isn't in itself a reason to call off the wedding. Bachelors traditionally have been very difficult when it comes to disentangling them from their mates. However, if he actually wants to take him into bed with you this should cause concern. Even if he says it's just to prevent the draught.

Catching him in *flagrante* with the bridesmaid would undoubtedly be a traumatic betrayal of your trust. On the other hand, if that lady is attractive, perhaps it's an inverted compliment to you that he's choosing you for his lifelong partner instead of her. What's important is to establish (a) if he wants to see her again, (b) if she's pregnant with his child and (c) if he wants her on the honeymoon as well as the best man. If (c) is the case, it would definitely be an idea to book a bigger hotel room.

Practical advice for weddings

From a hungry tiger and an affectionate woman there is no escape.

(Ernest Bramah)

Weddings. They're things people get married at right?

Wrong.

They're things people get piddled as newts at. Not to mention distraught, lachrymose, maudlin, obstreperous, obnoxious, naïve and royally, cancerously, monumentally and incurably bored.

How many weddings have you been at? Did you enjoy any of them? Come on, be honest. Four hours waiting for the meal to arrive, sitting through godawful speeches by people who say 'Unaccustomed as I am to Public Speaking' and sounding every inch of it, trying to say the Proper Things to people you abhor, and only starting to enjoy it after you get so drunk you're guaranteed not to remember it in the morning.

Weddings tend to go wrong before they've even started. Here we're concerned with those small little details that, while seemingly inconsequential to you, have the potential to turn a sunny afternoon in Sussex to a bad day in Beirut. Who to invite, who not to invite. Who will take umbrage, who will never speak to the family again if they don't get asked, who doesn't give a toss anyway (i.e. the intelligent ones).

Whatever you do, as all of us who have (mis)lived by Murphy's Law since first we saw the light of day, invariably turns out to be the wrong thing. X, who was asked, proves shambolical; Y who wasn't, is eternally peeved. Or else X and Y are both asked and go from bitchiness to fisticuffs after the third sherry.

You know the routine. The step-cousin from Slough, by some apocryphal oversight, ends up beside the Grimshaw grand-aunt she hasn't spoken to since 1965 because the former's brother-in-law had an argy-bargy with the latter's pet poodle one soggy Sunday.

So the excrement hits the proverbial ventilator as the conversation verges from how ravishing the bride is looking to what wonderful weather we're having for this time of year. After which all those nasty little gripes you've been assiduously building up for the past two decades hit home with a vengeance. It's at this stage in the proceedings that the extended family tends to jump in. Five minutes later you've got bodies splayed all over the place as if

Charles Manson has just left the building. The good news is that the Big Day is only that: a day. So you don't have to see all these vicious relatives and acquaintances until the next merry rendezvous.

It's slightly different if the bride and groom are at loggerheads, or if they've both realised they've made a horrible mistake about mid-way through the reception. This insight, you'll agree, could pose certain problems for their future together – or absence of it.

Should it upset the wedding day? Of course not. Wedding days are orchestrated towards the happiness of the guests and no one else. The misery of the bride and groom, if such exists, is carefully camouflaged under such time-honoured rituals as the throwing of the bouquet, the removing of the garter from the bride's leg – where on earth did that come from? – and so many hours spent listening to testimonials to people's character (usually rogues), you find yourself almost wishing you were at the Tory Party Conference.

I said *almost.*

I wanted to marry her ever since I saw the moonlight shining on the barrel of her father's shotgun.
(Eddie Albert)

Anyway, when all the frivolities are over and the woosome twosome trail off to their secret hideaway amidst the clattering of tin cans to fenders and the bronchitic wheeze of heartbroken dads downing their thirty-ninth vodka, somewhere a real future is born.

Life is about living, not exchanging pleasantries with

people you haven't seen for the last seventeen years and aren't likely to see for the next seventeen either. It's not about praising bad cooking or gushing about bridesmaids' dresses or taking advantage of the horny bachelor who happened up from Cornwall for the day.

Marriage is a wonderful invention, but then
so is the bicycle repair kit.
(Billy Connolly)

We've already touched on the subject of sex, but you might be interested to hear what a gentleman called Michael Green has to say on the subject vis-à-vis the wedding day.

'There is a problem' he points out 'that perhaps half the male guests have slept with the bride. Maybe the only one who hasn't is the groom.' This leads to logistical problems. 'All guests who've had sex with the bride must be placed on the groom's side. It's not fair to have a solid phalanx of young men all down the side of the church behind the bride, together with her boss and the sales manager.'

Greene, who seems to know an awful lot about this kind of thing, goes on to inform us that 'the best man always seems to be one of the bride's former lovers, while the groom has usually been in bed with a couple of the bridesmaids'. He also suggests that girls who have slept with the groom should sit on the bride's side.

Finally, Greene points out 'If the groom and the best man have slept together, cancel the wedding.'

The mourning after the Knot before

The success of the marriage comes after the failure of the honeymoon.

(G. K. Chesterton)

Honeymoons are traditionally supposed to be those times in our lives when all our frustrated sexual longings finally come to fruition. Does it always happen like that? Make up your own mind as you sample the following debâcles.

When Catherine the Great of Russia went to her boudoir on the night of her wedding she discovered that her husband was more interested in playing with his toy soldiers over the sheets than anything else between them. A girl called Audrey Letton, in more recent times, experienced similar feelings of *coitus interruptus* – or rather *coitus non-existus* – when she found the Welsh hotel she was to honeymoon in had only single beds. Not to be outdone, she grabbed her husband and hotfooted it back to her own (double-bedded) home with these brave words: 'I can't wait; I've been saving myself.' Isn't it a fine thing to know that the things you really want in life are the same?

On the other end of the scale, Lord Charles Beresford, who married at the beginning of the century, was somewhat over-zealous on the night of his honeymoon and burst in to what he thought was his bride's room with cries of 'Cock-a-doodle-do!' It was only moments later, as he lay splayed across the bed, that he realised he was surrounded by the Bishop of Chester and his wife.

The wife of Henbury soccer player Mike Cox had similar bad luck on the first morning of her honeymoon when Mike was dragged out of his marital bed to play a game, the original team having got too drunk at the reception the day before. It was a classic case, as one sports commentator put it, of leaving the bride with sweet FA. This is nothing in comparison to the Indian couple who, both being ignorant of the facts of life on their wedding night, were reduced to knocking on the door of the bride's mother to find out what to do.

A honeymooning Irishman called Philip Ryan fell 500 feet to his death in a volcano on an Indian Ocean island in 1977 when a fence he vaulted turned out to be leading into something he didn't quite expect. Equally hapless was David Bryant, who was having his bride photograph him as he stood on the edge of a cliff. He toppled over the edge and fell 50 feet into the Avon gorge. His wife was zooming in on his terrified face as he fell but the camera was out of focus so she thought he was smiling. Someone said it gave a whole new meaning to 'falling' in love.

Wives suffer too. A Greek bride's marital bliss was short-lived when the pins that a seamstress had mistakenly left in her wedding-gown penetrated her bottom. She was unable to sit down for the duration of the wedding reception. This is one of the things they don't tell us to watch out for in pre-marriage courses. She still got off lighter than Richard Hopkins, who was honeymooning in Barbados when a speedboat ran him over, gashing his bum so badly he had to have 19 stitches. He spent the rest of his 'holiday' lying on his front.

When Tony and Madge Reilly were at their wedding reception, a champagne bottle fell off a table and exploded, showering Madge with broken glass. She had to be rushed to hospital and her leg encased in plaster. She commented afterwards, 'Tony did promise to love me in sickness and in health, but I don't think he expected it to be this soon.'

A similar catastrophe befell a man who was on his way to a railway station after the wedding reception. His mates decided that, being the day that it was, they'd lift him up and toss him in the air a few times for the crack. The crack took on another meaning when he crashed to the ground and set off on his honeymoon semi-conscious. With friends like that … .

A doctor who got hellaciously drunk at his wedding, fell prey to perhaps the greatest trick of all. His friends encased his leg in plaster after he went to sleep and told him the next morning that he'd broken it the day before. He'd booked a honeymoon in Switzerland and still went there, but spent the whole fortnight shivering as he watched his wife ski over the snow. The overall diagnosis? A man who got 'plastered while plastered'.

A gentleman called Robert Neidheisrer was even more unlucky: he breathed his last breath in Pennsylvania only moments after uttering the words: 'I do.' This is probably the shortest wedding on record, but there have been some pretty brief honeymoons too. Eva Gabor commented thus on her third husband, plastic surgeon John Williams, 'After we were married one minute, I wanted to leave him.' Which isn't really flattering to the groom, when you think about it.

Even worse was the situation of Marisa Carlotta, who met an old flame at her wedding, chatted to him for a while and, realising she still loved him, took off with him to New York there and then.

New Zealand-born writer Katherine Mansfield's 'wedding' lasted somewhat longer: all the way to the honeymoon hotel in fact. Once there she took a dislike to the decor of her room and vamoosed. The man who said women were made to be loved rather than understood may have had a point.

Barbara Hutton's honeymoon actually did get started, but once she divested herself of her trousseau and slipped into something more comfortable, as brides are wont to do, the first words out of her husband's mouth were, 'Barbara, you are too fat.' Compare this to what happened to writer Al Alvarez when he took breakfast up to his sleeping bride the morning after the night before. 'It's a lovely morning,' he said as she bit into her toast. Then a look of some dismay came into her face as she said, 'You didn't cut off the crusts.' Mr Alvarez is a man who has attempted suicide; I hope there's no connection.

Pity the plight of insurance broker Ken Simkin who woke up one morning next to an eighteen-stone blonde called 'Big Mama' only to find that he'd married her the previous day in the course of a drunken binge. The incident, he felt, had one positive side effect: it put him off drink for life.

You've probably read about the incident some years ago

when Ian Botham's athletic endeavours in the boudoir are alleged to have caused the bed to collapse. In Majorca in 1980, hoteliers complained that honeymooners were costing them £1,000,000 a year in bed repairs, one couple having achieved the dubious honour of buckling four bedsprings in a fortnight. This would have been acceptable to the said hoteliers except for the fact that their insurance companies refused to compensate them for repairs. The damage lovemaking does to beds comes under the heading 'wear and tear' in their book, and isn't covered by insurance. So now the hotels bear this somewhat ambiguous slogan: 'Before making love, please consider the landlord.'

Which isn't to suggest that excessive passion at moments like this is peculiar to our own age. In the year 453, Attila the Hun is alleged to have become so excited by his new bride that he died of a burst artery. The word in biographical circles is that 'he came and went'. Boom, boom. While Richard the Lionheart, choosing to get married in the exotic location of Cyprus, proceeded to spend his eighty-day honeymoon rampaging across the island and finally forcing its king to surrender it to him. Talk about a wedding gift!

Astronomer Edmond Halley didn't share Attila's resolve, spending most of his honeymoon looking for comets. I hope they weren't the kind that only appear every eighty years or I wouldn't have given much chance of his betrothed enjoying a fulfilled matrimonial life. At Cesare Borgia's wedding someone slipped a laxative into his bubbly and he spent most of the night communing with a different kind of nature than he may have imagined.

In London some time ago a bridegroom ended up in court because he broke into a contraceptive machine on his wedding night. It appears his lady wife refused to let him into the boudoir without same. He was fined £25 but I'm sure he thought it was worth it.

I don't know if you could say the same for Arthur Milbank. He was in the middle of a passion session when his mattress caught fire, and not being exactly in form for spending time dousing it (in case it doused his ardour too) he chucked it out the window. The mattress then also set the garden ablaze, and moments later the fire brigade were hammering at the door.

I'm sure there's a moral for all of us: don't smoke when making love. Though considering a modern romantic has been defined as someone who removes a cigarette from his mouth while kissing his wife, that's surely going to be easier said than done.

In another incident a bride and groom had their first marital flare-up when the latter decided he didn't like her choice of green curtains. They had words together and he ended up storming out of the house. A moment later his wife, deciding she felt sorry for him, leapt out of her second-floor window on top of him. All ended well, though. She only broke her neck and his leg … and they were fortunate enough to receive adjoining hospital beds.

So many things went wrong for Karen and Steve Price in

the run-up to their wedding that they decided to stay at home for their honeymoon. First of all the firm from which she ordered her wedding dress went bust. She eventually managed to retrieve it from the bailiff's warehouse. They then hired a Rolls Royce as a bridal car and that was vandalised. When the bridesmaid's dresses arrived they were the wrong size and had to be re-made. Finally, the caterer fell ill and couldn't prepare the wedding feast. Are you surprised they weren't taking any chances with the honeymoon?

Maybe the most unlikely honeymoon of all concerned 10th century King Ethelred, who was found on his wedding night in bed with both his wife and his mother-in-law. Come again? I dunno ... maybe he was a feminist before his time. Or adopting a novel approach to warding off in-law problems.

Sometimes honeymoons are characterised not so much by what transpires between the Happy Couple as those who they have to carry along the way. We've all heard about the mama's boy who wanted to bring his mother with him, but what would you make of Barry Hodkin, who insisted on taking no less than thirty of his boozing pals from the local pub. He said to his wife afterwards, 'I've been married four times and this was my best honeymoon.' Which raises all sorts of questions. Marie Dudding from Berkshire went one better – or worse. She spent her honeymoon with her husband ... and 29 rugby players.

Maybe not too surprising after all this that one long-suffering mother was heard to comment 'If you survive the honeymoon, anything – even marriage – is easy'. I think this is what you call Positive Thinking.

So while you're stuck indoors on your honeymoon because it's raining, desperately missing your mates and the pub, trying to ignore the fact that what you're trying to eat is still moving, remember that comparativly, you're doing really well.

How to Know when the honeymoon is over

We sleep in separate rooms, we have dinner apart, we take separate vacations – we're doing everything we can to keep our marriage together.
(Rodney Dangerfield)

Okay, let's set the stage for the average marriage. You've fallen in love with him at first – or maybe second – sight. He looks to have all the proper attributes: two hands, two legs, and a face that has a nose, a mouth and two matching eyes. Well you can't be too choosy. Also, he seems to be relatively house-trained and can be safely invited over to Aunt Bertha's without barfing all over the kitchen after the hors d'oeuvres.

So he produces the sparkles and you say yes, contemplating fifty years of wedded bliss.

Except it doesn't quite work out like that. In fact no sooner are you out of your bridal gown than he says something like 'What have you done to your hair?' And then, on the plane to the Algarve for your 'magical' (ha ha) fortnight, just after belching into the in-flight chicken nuggets, he tells you that he's despised your entire family since he first clapped eyes on them. After which he asks you to pass him the salt.

When you arrive at the hotel, you cry niagarous tears into all the telegrams that promised moonlight and roses. Meanwhile, your betrothed is downstairs in the lounge with his newly-acquired drinking mate Pedro, getting seriously blotto on a raft of dodgy liqueurs.

Two weeks later (I haven't mentioned anything about the wedding night because you know about that already) you come back to the little semi-detached house in Berwick-upon-Tweed (which you won't own until you're about eighty-seven because he's just got demoted in his job and you had to go for that 'shorter-paying-mortgage with the longer-time-span-plan') and the problems continue. He's out most of the time and when he isn't you start to feel worse. Uh-oh. You tell your mother and she says 'All men are like that. You'll get used to it'. (Thanks, Mum). Then your father chips in with, 'The first twenty years are the worst' – consolingly.

The main problem with women is they get all excited about nothing – and then marry it.
(Cher)

Welcome back to the real world. This is where you fully discover that your sophisticated, tall, dark and handsome Hugh Grant is actually Fred Flintstone in disguise. The shirts from the Savoy Tailors will go, as will the smart trousers. He'll start dressing like the Missing Link and acting accordingly. He'll cheer when he hears the latest exploits of Liam Gallagher or Vinnie Jones and look confused when you try to talk to him about anything other than football, cars or beer.

If you can manage to persuade him to take you out for the night, you'd better take out a life-insurance policy before he decides to take you on to the dance floor. He moves like a sponsored epileptic fit and will grope you in a manner that suggests at least a dozen pairs of hands. During the slow set he'll put his tongue so far down your throat you'll expect to see it coming out of your toes.

I married beneath me. All women do.
(Nancy Astor)

Finally you'll realise why he's brought you to this club as he takes you to the bar and re-introduces you to all his mates that you met briefly at the wedding and hoped never to see again. They will all have names like Jimmy or Larry, or anything ending with 'y'. He may refer to you as his 'squeeze'. In this case the term will have literal ramifications as he simultaneously shows you off and asserts his proprietorial rights over you.

As soon as he has consumed sufficient quantities of lager (washed down with chasers) he'll steer you back towards your love-nest. Fortunately you won't have

to make too many protestations that you don't want to have sex with a drunken gorilla. The headache line will work after a few minutes when he gets bored and passes out. Fortunately this excuse is as old as stone-age woman and so, having been told it so often and for so long, the stone-age man knows better than to argue.

If you ever make the mistake of asking him to cook, don't be surprised by the appearance of two TV dinners and a can of cheap lager. You might be surprised by his manners when he doesn't open said can with his teeth. Your surprise will be short lived as he punctures the bottom of one of the cans and shotguns it down his throat and then, like a true gentleman, offers to do the same for you.

His taste in music has also radically altered from the smoochy love-songs that you like to anything that reaches and breaches the hundred decibel mark. Complaining neighbours are only a matter of time and his response will be to turn the sound up, leaving you to deal with the increasingly irate cohabitants of your street.

Wife 1: How's the pain in the neck these days?
Wife 2: Oh it's alright. He's gone off with his mates
for a few days.

The reason for this transformation is simple. Before marriage he had to impress you. Now you've bound yourself to him for life, which means he can make lewd comments to you with impunity and force you to listen to his crap, inane and insensitive jokes. It's a good idea to prepare yourself for this transformation and be ready for when it occurs. It will be a gradual decline and may be halted if caught early enough. The trick is not let yourself bask in the newly-wed glow, but get straight on to the toilet training.

Problems with relationships and how to solve them

Never go to bed angry. Stay up and fight.

(Anon.)

Women are strange; intractable creatures and, unfortunately, marriage doesn't alter this fact. There are a number of situations that can flare up into full-scale rows if not handled correctly. Follow our brief guidelines to avoid the worst.

Problem 1: She feels you don't love her as much as you used to.
Solution: No-one is really sure what this means. However, learn some Shakespearean sonnets and at Valentine's Day reel them off while delivering a card that's bigger (and more expensive) than your house. Whisk her off to San Francisco and bungee jump off the Golden Gate Bridge to demonstrate your undying love for her. Alternatively this can be interpreted as a call for you do more housework. Empty the dishwasher occasionally.

Problem 2: You forgot her birthday.
Solution: Don't worry, after she's finished with you, you won't ever forget it again.

Problem 3: She feels you ignore her in company.
Solution: Easily resolved, simply spend the whole party attending to every drink need and dance whim while ignoring all others in the room. If Kate Winslet or Jennifer Aniston are also at the same party a cold shower may be appropriate beforehand.

Problem 4: She feels that you're too needy and clingy and she wants her own space.
Solution: Kate Winslet, Jennifer Aniston? Wehey!

Problem 5: You snore in bed.
Solution: Consult your doctor for, while this may sound trivial to you, at three in morning it's the most important thing in the world to your wife and may be grounds for divorce. Failing a simple medical solution, separate rooms for sleeping may be an interim measure.

The best way to get rid of noise in a car is to let her drive.
(Oliver Hereford)

Problem 6: She feels you're leading separate lives.
Solution: Take her complaint on board. Examine how many friends you have in common, what things you do together and so on. Try to synchronise your work/leisure schedule to fit in with hers. Don't have two TVs in the house and make sure you always eat together. Above all, you had better find out which room she's sleeping in and move back in.

Problem 7: She's worried about money.
Solution: Do not point out how much she spent on a dress for our Lisa's wedding. Reassure her that there's always a way out of financial difficulty, second-mortgage your house, upgrade your job, downgrade your lifestyle (but not hers). Do not at any point imply that it is in any way her fault.

Problem 8: She feels fat and dowdy.
Solution: The female brain is hardwired with this belief and it will raise it's head every few months or with the purchase of a new dress. Buy lots of headache pills to prepare for the hour-long tirade you'll receive on the state of her thighs.

Problem 9: She feels that you're no longer sexually attracted to her.
Solution: Take a trip to Ann Summers (educational and fun) to buy her some kinky underwear and then cancel your subscription to *Playboy*.

There were no last words.
His wife was with him until the end.
(Spike Milligan)

However it is not always the female partner that may feel left out, ignored and unloved. Men can also suffer from exactly the same emotions and tend to retreat into their 'cave' when they feel unloved. So if you diagnose that your man is suffering from any of the aforementioned problems then here is what you should do:

Problem 1
Solution: Pamper his ego.

Problem 2
Solution: Pamper his ego.

Problem 3
Solution: Pamper his ego.

Problem 4
Solution: Pamper his ego.

Problem 5
Solution: Pamper his ego.

Problem 6
Solution: Pamper his ego.

Problem 7
Solution: Pamper his ego.

Problem 8
Solution: Pamper his ego.

Problem 9
Solution: Pamper his ego.

Psychologists like men a lot. They're simple and uncomplicated and much easier to handle than women.

Making the earth move

I know nothing about sex because I was always married.
(Zsa Zsa Gabor)

A woman who wasn't able to have sex with her husband because he had suffered severe injuries to his nether regions in an explosion sued him some years ago in Ireland and she was awarded £20,000 in compensation by the judge.

Is that too much? Is it not enough? And how, pray tell, do you evaluate these things? Was she asked under oath 'How was it for you?' and the damages evaluated accordingly?

The woman discovered testosterone injections for her other half after nine years and everything is now hunky dory, I believe, so the compensation figure was for the nine years when she had to, as she put it, 'bottle it all up'.

When I read about this unfortunate couple – her hapless husband also suffered 'a gross loss of tissue in the perineum and buttocks, and rupture of the scrotum' – it struck me how the world has changed. I mean, twenty or thirty years ago, there's many a put-upon Irish wife who would have prayed nightly that something of that nature would happen to her husband so that he'd stop crawling all over every night when he came home from work looking for a shag and his supper.

A change in the law in 1989 enabled this woman to sue the state for her years of deprivation, and rightly so. I've said it before and I'll say it again: these days (or rather nights) it's more likely to be the men rather than the women who are saying 'Not tonight Josephine' in the boudoir … because they have a headache. They are even beginning to fake orgasms as well.

And it's the women who are looking for what I recently heard referred to as their 'jungle rights'. The New Woman, far from being inhibited sexually, can't wait to get out of the traps. You'd better have your Viagra handy for these damsels if your powers are waning after a hard day at the office. They'll greet you at the door not with mom's apple pie but some strenuous tonsil-tennis and a plethora of adventurous gropes. If you ask them what you're doing for dinner, the reply may well be 'You're having it already.'

This type of female – rapacious, pro-active, Amazonian – brings her own 'protection' on a date, and I don't mean a bodyguard. She'll ask you to get her kit off faster than you can say 'Mary Whitehouse'. She'll encourage you to shop at Agent Provocateur for that extra special birthday prezzie which may cause you to age prematurely, and also develop breathing difficulties. She'll encourage you to flex you pecs, to tone up so that you can 'perform' in a manner that will meet her expectations (you'll be unable to exceed them) in the boudoir. If not, it's roll over Beethoven time. Or rather, 'Come out Andy Warhol, your fifteen minutes are up.'

Theoretically she's capable of raping you – but don't worry, you'll probably enjoy it. Leastways if she doesn't tie you up too tightly. In general she thinks of sex not so much as an expression of undying troth, as, well, aerobic exercise. And, as with all aerobic exercise, you have to be fit for it. So if you develop a gut, she's quite capable of kicking you out of the bed to make way for a younger model.

How does she spend her spare time? Tupperware parties? Carol Vorderman on the gogglebox? No, this damsel is more likely to be found at the local strip club stuffing tenners into the jockstrap of the latest Dolph Lundgren lookalike from Amsterdam as he dangles his wobbly bits in her face to the background din of the *The Full Monty*.

Truly gone are the days of 'Lie back and think of England' and 'Brace yourself Brigid' as Himself came home from the boozer, did the needful and then rolled over and went to sleep before his spouse was finished saying 'No, darling, you haven't got the spot just yet.' And have you noticed the harried expression husbands have on their faces when their other halves mention 'We're trying for a baby'? This will involve manic amounts of sex. Which on the face of it, is great. Unfortunately it will also involve charts, optimal timing, humiliating visits to the doctor to have a sperm count and that sinking feeling in the pit of your stomach that makes you feel like your gonads have gone AWOL.

Toilet training

*Man is a domestic animal which, if treated with firmness
and kindness, can be trained to do most things.*

(Jilly Cooper)

One of the most important things in married life is toilet
manners. A bleat beloved of feminists is that the men in
their lives, after visiting the little boy's room (and don't
feminists tend to see most men as semi-permanent little
boys?) invariably leave the toilet seat up. This, to their way
of thinking, is an offence commensurate with serial
killing or necrophilia.

I was reading an
interview with a guy
who's a certified 21-
carat barbaric chau-
vinist. In the course
of the interview, how-

*Give a woman an inch and she
will park a car on it.*
(E. P. B. White)

ever, he happened to mention (shock horror) that he
doesn't leave the loo seat up after doing his business. The
interviewer (who held decided feminist views) was emi-
nently chuffed. Does this mean we're approaching an age
where men can abuse/hit/terrify/terrorise/brutalise the
women in their lives but as long as they put the lavvy seat
down they're AOK with the PC brigade?

Looking at it from the other end of the spectrum, is
putting down the loo seat the thin end of the wedge?
Once you've given in on this one, what will you have
to do next time? In the war of the sexes the toilet seat is
the most hotly-contested battlefield. The question is:
is it a battle you can afford to lose? Of course there's the

argument that if they want the loo seat down, fine, it stays down. All the time. And if they complain about the resulting mess? Well they did ask for it.

These women also seem to be completely unaware that perhaps we men don't like having our bathroom covered with semi-empty shampoo bottles of several different varieties from dandruff-free to colour-rich enhancer. Not to mention the conditioner, cleansing skin wash, foaming body wash, hair-dye, moisturiser, moisturising face-balm, exfoliating lotion and the mandatory sixteen types of different coloured fruit-shaped soaps and assorted smellies. If you ask me, bathroom manners runs both ways. And why do women insist on going to the loo and leaving the door open? Do they think we're fetishists? Do they think we all want to listen to them doing their business? I'm all for intimacy, but really.

A personal experience of the institution

The woman cries before the wedding, and the man after.
(Polish proverb)

I got married some time ago. I can't remember exactly when. It seems like years but I know it's only months. Wives do things like that to you. My old friends meet me on the street and say 'You look different.' What they mean is 'older' but they're too polite to say that, being friends. They think I might be offended. I wouldn't though; I know what's causing it too. Metal fatigue.

I once used to gloat at all those holiday postcard gags with fat overbearing wives and wimpy henpecked husbands. I thought they were a great joke. Now I'm beginning to realise the awful truth. We're all wimpy and henpecked. Even Schwarzenneger probably suffers from it if I know anything. None of us are safe. 'He that has a wife, has a master' is an old Scottish saying.

A husband is what's left of a lover after the nerve has been extracted.
(Helen Rowland)

In a civilised world, you might ask, why do they carry on like this? Live and let live is my philosophy. But it's getting harder to adhere to. If you're planning to take your woman to the altar in the near – or even distant – future, I would seriously ponder the following points about wives.

(1) They tend to get narky if you roll in the door drunk – even at weekends, which is a bit hard to take.

(2) They don't like to see you chatting up other women at parties.

(3) They blow a fuse if they see you out with another woman.

(4) They have a low threshold of boredom as you rabbit on about what happened in the office during the day. This is in marked contrast to your dating days, when they hung on your every word. Conversely, if you don't listen to them you're asking for trouble.

(5) They're always going on about the house being filthy instead of doing something about it.

(6) Even after coming home knackered from your 40-hour week, they expect you to do your share of the dishes. The overture to this is usually something like 'This is a 50-50 marriage, you know.' When you hear this kind of baloney it's time to bale out: they've obviously been reading the wrong kinds of books – probably by Andrea Dworkin.

(7) When they get into their 'purple' moods after a few too many glasses of vino, they tend to come out with things like 'I want my own emotional space.' When I hear this kind of talk I know the kind of space I feel like giving them – a night out on the front lawn with all the doors bolted and locks changed. I'm sure that would cure it all right.

(8) They don't bring you your slippers anymore. 'Modern Thinking' dictates that it's demeaning for a woman. God spare me from Modern Thinking.

If you think women are the weaker sex, try pulling the blankets over to your side of the bed.
(Stuart Turner)

I hope you read the above with great care before taking any rash steps as I think I speak for all husbands about my disenchantment. It wouldn't be so bad if the said women telegraphed their transmogrification in advance. But no. In the dating days they drool over your sweaty armpits and smelly socks as if you're a latterday Kowalski. After marriage all they do is moan about when you're going to leave your animal ways behind you. Being the true-blue gent you are, you refrain from reminding them that they once found such animalism a right little turn-on.

Marriage is based on the theory that when a man
discovers a brand of beer exactly to his taste,
he should at once throw up his job and
go work in the brewery
(George Nathan)

As if that wasn't bad enough, you have to put up with them cutting their toenails in bed and sitting around the TV of an evening painting them with foul-smelling concoctions. In the bathroom you continue your daily ritual of pulling their hair out of the plughole in great lumps so you can let the water out of the bath.

The greatest sin of all is when you have a few mates round for the evening. If it gets lively in the slightest way or the neighbours start complaining, they go up the wall. All over a few innocent rugby songs or some such diversion. They spend most of their time moaning about the beer stains on the carpet instead of entering into the spirit (forgive the pun) of things. My own philosophy is that if you're going to be a killjoy in life then get thee to a nunnery.

Minority rules

I have good-looking kids. Thank goodness my wife cheats on me.

(Rodney Dangerfield)

If you're happily married, i.e. if you belong to that 1% of the population, the next question is whether to have children. Of course there may be some of you who had to get married *because* you were having children. If this is the case then you have neatly avoided all the following issues by jumping the gun. Here, in any case, are the immutable laws of parenting:

(1) If your wife wants children, you won't and vice versa.

(2) If she wants a daughter, you'll want a son. If she wants a son, you'll want a daughter.

(3) If you both want a daughter, you'll have a son.

(4) If you both want a son, you'll have a daughter.

(5) If you practice birth control so she'll only get pregnant once, then it will be twins, triplets or worse.

The last time you'll be perfectly happy with your baby is the first time you're with it, when you take it in your arms at the hospital. After that, it's all downhill.

Babies are crying machines and pooing machines. They don't tell you this in the textbooks. They don't tell you that when you have one, you're signing up for semi-permanent insomnia for about three years, give or take. When a baby utters its first word, make sure you're there to hear it, though with today's environment it will probably be a four-lettered one. Also witness its first step: probably into wet cement.

As a child grows, you can witness the wonders of its discovery experiences: discovering how to throw laptops down the toilet bowl; discovering how to boil jewellery in a saucepan; discovering how passports and driving licenses burn when you set them alight.

When it goes to school, the little dear, you'll almost miss it wrecking the house. You'll be nostalgic for anarchy. Life, suddenly, will lose some of its allure. You'll not quite be able to cope with the surprise of coming home and finding everything just like you left it. In no time at all, the man who has insured your home and effects will learn to smile again, contrary to your belief that that part of his face was paralysed into a grimace.

A bitch loves being born. It's her first experience of making another woman scream and cry and she likes it.
(Pamela Anderson)

It's only a short journey from here to puberty. The signal for this is your darling bringing many strange people to the house, people who look at you as if to say. 'What are you doing here?' This is what sociologists call 'peer group pressure', and what parents call something much more obscene.

At this point of your child's life, any questions you ask them will be greeted by responses like: 'What?', 'Uh?', 'No, that's not true', 'I didn't do it', 'Why should I clean my room?', 'Why don't I get paid for going to school?', 'I didn't ask to be born', 'You keep saying that, shut up', 'We've been through this before', 'Get a life', 'Butt out', 'Get off my case', and perhaps most endearingly: 'Why don't you drop dead and do us all a favour'.

110

But it's not all bad. There are a few seminal moments in a young persons' life that make parenthood all worthwhile. There's nothing quite like the warm fuzzy glow you get when you see your child do something for the first time. For a boy these tend to be:

Age 2:   Learns to walk.

Age 3:   Learns to break things.

Age 4:   School. Seeds of anti-authoritarianism.

Age 7:   First suspension.

Age 9:   Awkward questions about where he came from.

Age 10: More sophisticated awkward questions that he already knows the answers to.

Age 17: Leaves school and gets his first job. (First day: 'Shall I wrap them up or are you having them here?')

Age 18: Runs away from home. Back the same night 'cos he missed supper.

Age 19: Meaningful existential discussions about life and shagging. Followed by a kebab with extra chili sauce. Lots of male bonding in late-night pubs and rave discos.

Age 20: Tells you you know nothing about life but still wants you to provide him with weekly pocket money.

Age 21: Big into DVDs, the internet and tantric sex.

Age 22: Moves out of house to live with girlfriend. Back each weekend for more dosh.

Age 23: Gets so bladdered he has to learn to walk again.

Which is were we came in …

There's just one pretty child in the world.
Every mother has it.
(Anon.)

Many people have already decided that this it too much and are becoming DINKIES: that's Double Income No Kids. It makes economic sense and also does wonders for your mental health. Remember Doris Day's comment: 'Insanity is hereditary; you get it from your children.' Compare that with Lionel Kaufman's: 'Children are great comforters in old age, and they also help you to reach it faster.' Although Fields opined that anyone who hates children and animals can't be all bad.

However if you still refuse to hear the voice of wisdom then remember: they're not returnable. Jack Lemmon used to say that they were like waffles: the first one should be thrown out. Maybe the RSPCC wouldn't approve of that.

Whatever you do, make sure your progeny is planned, and doesn't come from the bottom of a whiskey bottle. No, don't tell me it wouldn't fit there. What I'm trying to say is that people usually say most accidents are caused by children, but the reality of the situation is that most children are caused by accident.

Parenthood doesn't come with a book of instructions so you have to learn it the hard way. The secret is not to try and impose yourself over your children. Admit defeat from Day One and they will be much easier to bear. Above all remember that home is a hard hat area, so if you find them trying to put the VCR into the washing machine or the hamster into the microwave 'because it was cold' take it on the chin. Such minor trials will strengthen your relationship to your loved one.

Alternatively you could listen to Victoria Billings, who said that the best thing that could happen to motherhood already has: fewer women are going into it. You would probably agree that the only time a woman wishes she were a year older is when she's pregnant. Then again only if she hasn't heard of the new fad that's taking America by storm whereby children are thinking of divorcing their parents, and vice versa. Cloris Leachman was certainly being prophetic when she said 'I think husbands and wives should live in separate houses. And if there's enough money, the children should live in a third one.' Talk about a nuclear family.

Maybe Quentin Crisp put his finger on the central issue besetting juveniles when he said, 'The young always have the same problem: how to rebel and conform at the same time. They have now solved this by defying their parents and copying one another.' It's true, isn't it – many of the younger generation are alike in so many disrespects, giving rise to the line 'I'm a non-conformist – like everyone else!' or declaring that they are going to demonstrate against globalisation in the May Day riots, and join the International Solidarity to do so.

An even more irksome feature of the younger generation is their precociousness. If you see a parent sitting down for a *tête-à-tête* with their offspring these days, it's more often to learn than to teach. Anthony Powell's comment was particularly poignant: 'Parents are often a disappointment to their children – they don't fulfil the promise of their early years.' Or J. M. Barrie's equally astute remark 'I'm not young enough to know everything.'

All this may make you feel that youth is wasted on the young. Or that it would be an ideal state if it came later in life. Did you know that more money is being spent on children's toys today than was spent on their parent's education?

They also carry a fair (or foul) amount of the folding stuff in their pockets … and the devil will find work for monied hands. Today toys, tomorrow booze, and maybe Ecstasy the day after that. Cue Pope of Trash John Waters for an insight: 'Twenty years ago smart kids took drugs to think more. Now stupid kids are taking them not to think, period.'

Before you open a vein about this dystopian state of affairs, you might take some small solace from the fact that in the future, what with the genome theory, stem cell research and so on, children will probably be cloneable. If so you'll be able to programme them to do anything at all – just like your video recorder. (Of course you'll have to get a non-programmed child to teach you how to use that first!)

Keeping the spark alive

Marriage is the best magician there is. In front of your eyes it can change an exciting, cute little dish into boring dishwater.

(Ryan O'Neal)

Is it as good as it always was? Do you still buy him presents for no reason? Do you feel shivery all over when you kiss? Or are you drifting indissolubly apart? Is your marriage a ropey one? Are nerves getting frayed too often? Worse still, have dishy men on the street started turning your head?

It may be time to start evaluating exactly where you're at – or not at. Listed below is a series of situations we all find ourselves in with our Other Halves at one time or another. Stressful yes, insurmountable NO! For pressure isn't half as important as how we cope with pressure. How would you react if the following situations occurred to you? Tick off the most appropriate answer and, at the end, add up your tally. You may be surprised at how far down the slippery slope you've come. Disasters tend to creep up on us rather than being instant explosions.

Can the slide be stopped? Of course it can. But the first step to cure is accurate diagnosis. 'Know thyself', the Greeks said – and it still holds.

Situation One
He tells you you're too possessive. You're shocked. Do you:
(a) Let him out more so that he can have his own emotional space?

(b) Say 'Wouldn't it be worse if I ignored you'?
(c) Cut off his fingers one by one?

Situation Two
He says you're not giving him enough attention. Do you:
(a) Cut down on your workload and arrange a holiday away for both of you?
(b) Tell him you'll see him for a chinwag next Tuesday week at 4?
(c) Buy him a dummy and a pair of rompers and go 'Goochy, goochy goo'?

Situation Three
Your mother-in-law calls round for an evening. Do you:
(a) Talk the hind legs off both of them and be a model hostess?
(b) Lock yourself in your room and brood?
(c) Explode in a rage, saying 'I knew he had to have his nasty origins somewhere and now it's all beginning to make sense. And since the two of you seem to get on so well together maybe you both better spend the night together.'

Situation Four
You're both working until lights out and your leisure life has taken a hammering. One night he comes home dejected and tells you 'You're no fun anymore, not like the old days'. Do you:
(a) Work hard at playing hard for his benefit?
(b) Say 'What's funny about life, honeybun?'
(c) Tell him you have a terminal disease, which perhaps explains the fact that you haven't been the life and soul of the party lately?

Situation Five

You find him in bed with another woman. Do you:

(a) Examine your conscience to find out where you might be going wrong?

(b) Kick them both out of the house?

(c) Buy a double-barrelled shotgun and do the full (alleged) O. J.?

Now comes the hard bit – totting up your score. For every (a) you ticked, give yourself four points. For every (b), give yourself two points. For every (c) you get nothing. Well what did you expect?

If you scored between fifteen and twenty points you can relax, your marriage is hunky dory and you both deserve gold medals. If you scored between ten and fifteen, things are a bit iffy. Work on it. Try to find out what his deeper needs are. Give yourself a pep talk and tell yourself that life would be terminally boring if he was too lovey-dovey all the time. Get in touch with his 'sensitive' side. Don't ask where he got his appetite so long as he comes home for supper. Above all, realise that marriages are give and take. Sometimes one of you gives and the other takes. Perhaps he's feeling that he's been giving to much and has just shut down. Perhaps you do. Perhaps space is the answer. But don't stay away too long because he might not be there when you come back. If you got between five and ten you should look up all the divorce lawyers in the phone book. Or maybe hire a hit man.

To those of you who totalled less than five points ... go to a mountain, climb to the top. Scratch your navel. Contemplate where it all went wrong. Or tell the bastard it's all his fault. Believe me, this works every time.

Getting turned on

There are a number of mechanical devices which increase sexual arousal in women. Chief among these is the Mercedes-Benz 380 SL convertible.

(P. J. O'Rourke)

Since time immemorial people have been fascinated by aphrodisiacs. In the olden days tomatoes were brought to Europe from South America because these 'love apples' – as they were then called – were regarded as Forbidden Fruit. Others swore by lust inducers like baked potatoes, camel humps, oysters, bananas, cherries, peaches, pomegranates, asparagus, cucumbers, garlic and all sorts of peppers.

Aphrodite, the Greek goddess of Love, was born in the sea, which is a good reason why seafood has always been regarded in this light (or should it be darkness?) Over in America at the moment they're marketing a spray called Andosterone, which is made from a chemical secreted by

---

Someday my Prince will come.
However I'll have nothing to do with it.
(Anon.)

---

animals, which produces sexual responses in other animals. Specifically it's made, joking apart, from a musky substance secreted in the urine and saliva of a male pig. And it causes 'a sow in heat to stand in an arched mating position when a boar approaches'. I'm getting excited already.

But pig scent isn't the only option. Why not mail order latex briefs, fishnet stockings, exotic bras, creams and chastity belts and what about your very own willy-wammer. You can also get full value from magazines, working your way through articles like 'I Watched Him With a Neighbour', 'Flasher's Joy', 'I had thirty men in a day', 'Jodphur Jilly', 'Lust in the Dust' and 'Please Spank Me'.

Such magazines, we feel compelled to warn you, are also top heavy with nubile ladies in positions the Karma Sutra wouldn't have dreamed up. They look distinctly uncomfortable and one imagines a hefty sigh of relief was emitted from all concerned when the photographer shouted 'Cut!' and they were able to reclaim their legs from atop their cranium.

Last night I asked my husband what his favourite
sexual position was. He said 'Next door'.
(Joan Rivers)

If you dig a little deeper (strictly in the cause of research) you'll find things like 'Hard Up Harriet', 'I've Got It Licked' and if that doesn't get your motor going you can find a plethora of features on such delectable delights as All Girl Jelly Wrestling, Leather Rubber Girls (honest) and Sexy Submissive Wives.

My mother said it was simple to keep a man.
You must be a maid in the living room, a cook
in the kitchen, and a whore in the bedroom.
I said I'd hire the other two and take care
of the bedroom bit.
(Jerry Hall)

Truly gone are the days when foreplay was a bunch of orchids and a sweet smile rather than a floosie with a cat o'nine tails in her hand getting ready for position number 267 as she spits an oyster onto her jackboots before getting ready to goosestep across your chest.

Elvis Presley, apparently, liked watching bikini-clad young girls wrestling with each other through a two-way mirror to get his jollies. When he got together with Priscilla he liked her to dress up as a schoolteacher and spank him for being a naughty boy.

'Man is born free', said Rousseau 'but everywhere he is in chains.' Unfortunately he didn't live long enough to appreciate the full ramifications his comments would have for the swinging '60s and thenceforward. The good man didn't even witness the phenomenon of the Page Three Girl.

However, nowadays, thanks to progress, freedom of speech and some artistic interpretation of a variety of decency laws, you can probably find something to jingle your bell. There's even a scientific community dedicated to facilitating the erection. Isn't the twenty-first century a wonderful time to be alive?

Chapter 4
Inquest

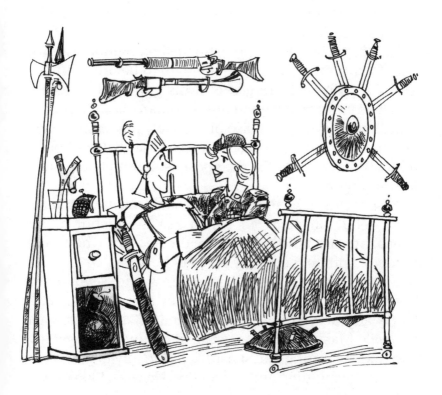

Better to have loved and lost than to have spent your whole life with the bastard.

(Anon.)

The wandering male

Get juiced up enough and you'll roll around with a buffalo and think she's beautiful.

(Lee Marvin)

Marriage is an institution. But who wants to live in an institution? A recent survey in America revealed that 66% of men had extra-marital sex. Why do men wander? because they're men!

The Ladykiller is to be distinguished by one essential character trait: he preserves the right to be unfaithful but blows a cylinder head gasket if his girlfriend or wife so much as looks sideways at another man. As well as being inordinately randy he's also obsessively possessive. He's a graduate of the do-what-I-say-not-what-I-do school of ethics. What's sauce for the goose is definitely not sauce for the gander.

'Never trust a husband too far' said Dorothy Parker 'or a bachelor too near'. To which Zsa Zsa Gabor added: 'Husbands are a little like fires: they go out when unattended.' And not generally alone either.

Marital fidelity, at the minute, would seem to be honoured more in the breach than the observance. In fact many people believe the plural of spouse is spice. Marcello Mastroianni once said: 'From my wife I get love and understanding and sensitivity; from my mistress I get love, understanding and sensuality.' He wasn't looking for much, was he?

Compare that to Joan Fontaine's comment: 'The main problem in marriage is that, for a man, sex is a hunger – like eating. And if he can't get to a French restaurant, he'll go to a hot dog stand.' Paul Newman would disagree. 'Why go out for a hamburger when you can have steak at home?' he says, apropos long-time wife and standby, Joanne Woodward. But there's a Freudian slip here because he's still comparing her to a piece of meat.

Carl Sandburg confessed, 'I ask for only four things out of life: to be out of jail, to eat regular, to get a little love at home, and a little on the outside.'

Which isn't to say wives don't feel the urge to stray either. When the aforementioned Zsa Zsa Gabor was asked how many husbands she'd had, she replied in inimitable Gaboresque fashion: 'You mean apart from my own?' Britt Ekland was a tad more tactless. 'When I say I sleep with married men' she explained, 'I mean *unhappily* married men.' It may be all the difference we need. Liz Taylor stated, by way of corollary, 'I've only slept with the men I've been married to. How many women can make that claim?' True, Liz, but then again, how many women can claim to be married a whopping eight times?

Even in our quote unquote enlightened era we still have an acute doublethink with regard to the kinds of sexual (mis)behaviour men are entitled to get up to, and that permissible to the 'gentle' sex. As one writer put it, 'Centuries of sanctioned male promiscuity have meant that the only recognised form of adultery was female adultery.' The male version hasn't only been licensed, but in many ways is a perceived staple of virility. Needless to say, there's no linguistic female equivalent to virility. And a man who plays around may be a bit of a lad, but a woman is an unconscionable slut.

The knock-on effect of such psychosexual tunnel vision is that a man who rejects a female overture risks having his virility doubted, whereas a woman who accepts one risks having her virtue called into question.

Thus, the skill and strategy of refusal is noticeably excluded from the family syllabus for boys, whereas it has long been a mandatory requirement for girls. Does this mean that a so-called 'liberated' woman is still whispered of as being 'easy' by laddish lager louts?

If a man is unfaithful to his wife, such doublethink makes itself even more apparent. The other woman in his life is inclined to say things like 'He wouldn't have asked me out if he wasn't unhappy' – without even asking him! In this way, a perfectly happy man's cheating is rationalised and endorsed without him having to open his mouth, or even having to deliver the classic line 'My wife doesn't understand me.'

If he does speak, he can be guaranteed to justify his actions by saying, 'You caught me unawares', or 'You seduced me – I wasn't looking for a woman.' Afterwards comes the 'I promise I'll leave my wife for you' phase, which is a bit like saying the cheque is in the post.

Mae West had no compunctions in this area at all. 'Can you imagine the embarrassment of being caught in bed with your husband?' was one of her favourite expostulations. Indeed, as far as Hollywood is concerned, we seem to be approaching an age where people get their names in the gossip pages by being monogamous. It's reminiscent of Tallulah Bankhead's: 'Who do I have to screw to get out of this business?'

Dan Greenburg was hugely magnanimous when he said 'I could never have sex with anybody who didn't respect my wife.' Truly, the age of chivalry isn't dead. Steve Martin echoed Mr Greenburg when he said, 'There's only one thing I couldn't forgive my wife for, and that's if she found me in bed with another woman.'

Some extra-marital flings, however, seem to give marriages a much-needed shot in the arm, stopping either or both parties from taking each other for granted. I know a man who calls his betrothed 'my present wife' to keep her on her toes. I heard of another couple who realised how crazy they were about one another only after she had a one-night stand with a mutual friend. I'm reminded of the old cartoon where a couple is spotted canoodling on the street and one bystander says to another: 'See – I told you they weren't married.'

Maybe it's a case of different strokes for different folks. Yves Montand used to say: 'A man is entitled to two, maybe three love affairs while he's married: after that he's cheating.' Such a sentiment seems to give the lie to the old adage that an open marriage is nature's way of telling you you need a divorce. Maybe 'ajar' would be a better term than 'open' in this instance, as far as Mr Montand is concerned.

John Updike had an unusual slant on the topic when he said that the first thrill of adultery was entering his mistress's' house because 'Everything has been paid for by the other man.' And then of course there's the geographical consideration. Updike probably hadn't heard the story of the Athenian taxi driver who received something of a fright when the man he stopped to pick up gave the taxi driver's address as his destination. When they got there, the man opened the door with a key he had in his pocket. A few minutes later the taxi driver followed him upstairs and found him in bed with his wife. The lesson is clear: don't commit adultery in another man's house. While a hotel may be more expensive, it's a damn sight safer.

My favourite quote on the subject is Rodney Dangerfield's poignant: 'I told my wife I was seeing a shrink. Then she told me she was seeing a shrink, a bartender and two plumbers!'

Revenge

Girls are dynamite. If you don't believe that, try dropping one.

(Hal Roach)

Brigitte Bardot held that it was better to be unfaithful than faithful without wanting to be, and I'll go along with that. Jackie Collins feels that it's primarily a male problem: 'Men are like little boys', she says, 'they want the bar of candy they can't have, and when they've got it they go out and look for another piece.'

The psychologist Carl Jung said that infidelity wasn't necessarily an unhealthy thing. In fact he believed that a license to be unfaithful was the prerequisite for a good marriage. Somerset Maugham would probably have agreed. He used to talk about the Tasmanians 'who never committed adultery, and are now extinct.'

There's an ideal woman for every man in the world, and he's damn lucky if his wife doesn't find out about her.
(Rodney Dangerfield)

Such wise words aside, if there's anything in the world that enrages people, more than infidelity – or even the suspicion of infidelity – I've never heard of it. If the situation arises in a marriage, the results can be extremely volatile. Apparently the first four minutes at the breakfast table and the first four minutes after arriving home from work are the flashpoints for three-quarters of all serious marital squabbles, according to an American psychologist. A further study concluded that women tend to kill their cheating husbands in the kitchen, whereas husbands prefer bedrooms when liquidating randy wives.

New Yorker Zaza Kimmont blew up when she walked into her bathroom one day and noticed a strange toothbrush next to her husband's. She flew into a rage when she noticed traces of lipstick on the bristles. She managed to cause £5,000 worth of damage as she threw everything breakable at the wall. Finally she stormed off to her mother … only to find that her mother-in-law had been to stay while she was away and had left her toothbrush behind. A salutary lesson for all.

It's hard to keep a wife in the dark when you're burning the candle at both ends.
(Henny Youngman)

A man called Evaristo, an eighty-five-year-old from fiery Sicily, went ape when he discovered a passionate billet doux addressed to his wife. Fearing the worst he stabbed her in the shoulder, but when he showed her the letter that suggested her infidelity, she pointed out that it was he who had written it fifty years previously. 'His sight was so poor that I forgave him,' she said rather magnanimously.

Prague housewife Vera Czermak wasn't quite so forgiving. She was so upset to find her husband cheating on her that she flung herself from the third floor window of her flat and landed on him in the street. When she regained consciousness in hospital she was informed that she was a widow.

The women who go to these sorts of lengths usually feel confident of success, the hubbie in question often having a track record of straying, or being suspected of it. Anyway, as we all know, men can resist everything except temptation.

One woman, who caught her boyfriend in a compromising position, sprayed water all over his carpet and then planted water cress seeds. Hey presto, instant swamp. Another said she ordered a builder to direct a stream of quick-set cement into the sunroof of her husband's car. Still another dropped her husband's toupee in a tin of red paint while he slept – then cut up his credit cards and put sugar in his petrol tank.

In a much-hyped infidelity case some years ago, gorgeous House of Commons research girl Pamella Bordes had a novel idea for getting her own back on her errant male – who just happened to be *Sunday Times* editor Andrew Neil. She hacked the crotches out of his megaexpensive suits (a metaphorical form of castration, one might think). Lady Sarah Moon, in similar vein, cut the arms off thirty-two of her rich husband's £1,000-apiece suits when he went straying. Not only that, but she poured five litres of paint on his BMW as well – and was generous enough to leave several bottles of his prize vino on the neighbours' doorstep to boot. Another woman more recently posted the details of her husband's infidelity on the internet, including the name and address of the woman with whom he had been playing away, as

---

Marriage is the only life sentence that can
be commuted for bad behaviour.
(Anon.)

---

well as other personal details. Nothing like sharing your problems to relieve the pain ... and ensure the very public humiliation of the wandering partner.

Another risk to infidelity is the fact that four out of five people who have heart attacks during lovemaking aren't married, says Dr Jean-Paul Broustet. When a middle-aged man makes love to his wife, according to Broustet, it's like climbing three floors ... but with his mistress it's like racing up the stairs of a skyscraper, or sprinting 3 miles.

If this isn't enough to deter you, bear in mind that Lorena Bobbitt isn't unique. In Thailand in 1985 an eighteen-year-old woman cut off her cheating husband's penis while he slept, a neighbour bringing the screaming man to hospital. The woman threw the offending organ out the window and when the doctor told a neighbour to retrieve it, he got there just as a covey of ducks were milling around it.

Of course it's not just men who cheat, despite what some might claim. It takes two to tango and men have a highly-developed ability for vengeance as well. In Sao Paulo, Brazil, a husband found his wife with another man and glued her hand to his penis with acrylic cement. Surgery managed to separate the body parts, but the man died a few days later from toxic poisoning because the cement had been absorbed into his bloodstream. A story to make the Glenn Close of *Fatal Attraction* look like she was just warming up.

We didn't invent sin, we're just trying to improve it.
(Anon.)

The beginning of the end

The term 'Divorce', comes from the latin 'Divorceum',
meaning 'To have your genitals torn out through
your wallet'.
(Robin Williams)

Not all relationships end with the doting couple retreating into the sunset, do they? If it wasn't for the acrimony and greed, divorce lawyers wouldn't be as mega-rich as they undoubtedly are.

People split up for as many reasons as they come together. An English judge granted a divorce to Doris and Albert May on the grounds of irreconcilable differences when their marriage broke down after twenty-six years. Albert alleged that Doris had charged him £4 each time they made love. Doris countered by saying that Albert ran around the house naked – and playing a tambourine – every time she rejected his advances.

This was similar to the hapless Wilhelm Stille, who was granted a divorce when he informed a Stuttgart court that he could no longer afford the 200 cigarettes and bottle of Schnapps which his wife charged him three times a week for love sessions.

Gene and Lynda Ballard opted for an unusual divorce in 1986 when the pair went freefall parachuting at 120 mph above California. Lynda's lawyer followed them out of the aircraft and served divorce papers on Gene at 12,000 feet. Then after a final mid-air kiss, they drifted apart (forgive the pun).

A Texas woman was once granted a divorce because of her husband's excessive tattooing. Not only did he cover her legs in anchors and cupids, he wanted to inscribe her back with the first verse of 'The Star Spangled Banner'.

A rich and sensitive man called Eugene Schneider objected when a divorce court judge in New Jersey ordered him to divide his property equally with his wife. When the judge insisted that the court order be carried out, Schneider took his chainsaw and cut his £40,000 wooden bungalow in half.

In the case of a German couple in 1985, divorce lawyers came up with an unusual solution to their problem by drawing up a two-year contract which prohibited the husband from doing any housework. Apparently he cooked the meals, brought his wife breakfast in bed, washed the dishes, put the children to bed, darned socks and still found time to go to work. His wife refused to sleep with him and filed for divorce. 'If only he'd go to the pub once in a while', she moaned, 'I can't stand a man who never does anything wrong.' A sentiment shared by most women, I'm sure. Otherwise what would we have to gossip and complain about?

If it's any consolation, even the celebrities have their share of problems. In fact celeb marriages are almost doomed to disaster from the outset. Considering that's the case, why do they keep making the same mistakes? 'Marriage is like the army,' said James Garner, 'everyone complains, but you'd be surprised at how many re-enlist.'

Lucille Ball married Desi Arnaz twice. Richard Burton and Liz Taylor did likewise, as did Natalie Wood and Robert Wagner. Stan Laurel was married eight times but only had four wives. Try and work that one out. Melanie Griffith lived with Don (*Miami Vice*) Johnson when she was sixteen, married him at eighteen, divorced him after four months, then married Stephen Bauer, then divorced him and then remarried Johnson in 1989. But she filed for

131

divorce from Johnson again in 1993. And you thought *your* marriage was complicated.

Celebs also love litigation. 'Love is generally valued at its highest,' said palimony pioneer Lee Marvin, 'during two periods in life: the days of courting and the days in court.' When Marla Maples assured everyone she was marrying Donald Trump for love rather than money, Jay Leno quipped 'Of course everyone knows you marry for love. You divorce for money.'

At the end of the day maybe we should bear Katharine Hepburn's words in mind. 'Sometimes I wonder if men and women really suit each other,' she emoted, 'perhaps they should live next door and just visit now and then.' That way they might avoid the sort of scenario Lily Tomlin alluded to when she said: 'I had a friend who was getting married, so I gave her a subscription to *Modern Bride*. The sub lasted longer than the marriage!'

There are the exceptions to marital discord, needless to say, but for every Gregory Peck or Paul Newman, there are innumerable Zsa Zsa Gabors and Liz Taylors. Or, to give her her full title, Elizabeth Taylor Hilton Wilding Todd Fisher Burton Warner Fortensky. Truly a set of surnames to be conjured with for the lady who said 'I do' eight times and assured us she meant it, every time.

Bette Davis was also married four times. So were Joan Collins, Frank Sinatra and Brigitte Bardot. Said Bardot after the last divorce, 'What attracts me in a man is his absence.' And thus saying she went from Women's Lib to Animal Lib.

Zsa Zsa Gabor was married eight times, insisting she was going to keep on doing it till she got it right. Rita Hayworth weighed in with seven husbands, as did Barbara Hutton and Jane Wyman. Richard Pryor and George C. Scott had 'only' five wives apiece while people like Ali MacGraw, Nick Nolte and Ava Gardner were almost monogamous with but three spouses each. Gardner's three husbands, however – Mickey Rooney, Artie Shaw and Frank Sinatra – clocked up a total of twenty wives between them.

'Fame cost me my family,' said the recently-jailed Robert Blake when his second wife Sondra Kerr left him, 'now I'm sleeping with a stranger called success'. Priscilla Presley claimed her marriage to Elvis failed because she couldn't give him the kind of adulation he got from his fans and needed desperately. 'Without it,' she said, 'he was nothing.'

Robin Williams' life has been something of a blitzkrieg thus far, and when he divorced Valerie Velardi he commented 'Right now I'm moving through my personal life like a haemophiliac in a razor factory.' How many other American film stars would know the feeling? After O.J. Simpson ended his first marriage he said philosophically: 'Life was good to me. I had a great wife, good kids, money, health ... but I was lonely and bored.' Prophetic words when viewed in the context of what happened to his second wife.

After Cher left Sonny, she married Greg Allmann. The liaison lasted a full nine days before she filed for divorce. The way things are going in Hollywood that might one day qualify as a lengthy marriage! Let's not forget Rudolph Valentino's first marriage lasted one day. And that Dennis Hopper was only married to Michelle Phillips eight days before they divorced. Burt Lancaster's marriage to June Ernst lasted a monumental one month.

Warren Beatty says he's found true love at last with Annette Bening, a surprising admission considering his legendary reputation for infidelity. Beatty claims he's mended his polygamous ways ever since he went From

There to Paternity, and who are we to argue.

Michelle Pfeiffer seems to be more interested in being a mother than a wife, as does Oprah Winfrey; both of these ladies pour scorn on all things matrimonial but dote over the idea of adopting children.

Julia Roberts ran away from the altar just twenty-four hours before she was due to say 'I do' to an unfaithful tearaway called Kiefer Sutherland and never regretted the decision: the part in *Runaway Bride* was perfect for her. She subsequently jumped the broom with the unlikely Lyle Lovett in a marriage that came to be known as Beauty and the Beast, though that went aground too. But they parted amicably so that's something at least. Now she's married again.

Sharon Stone has had a notorious reputation as a marriage wrecker for many years now, an allegation not helped by the fact that Bill McDonald, the executive producer of *Sliver*, left his wife for her before she dumped him in turn. Johnny Depp was engaged to Sherilyn Fenn and Jennifer Grey, and also to Winona Ryder, and yet broke off all three engagements to pursue model Kate Moss, before leaving her too.

Why do these people seem to keep making the same mistakes over and over again? Its a bit like doing 100 mph on the marital highway right after a blow-out. Or is it worth it, despite all the pain? I liked Peter de Vries' semi-masochistic piece of whimsy: 'I don't for the life of me understand why people keep insisting marriage is doomed. All five of mine worked out.'

Maybe it's the institution that's at fault rather than the people in it. 'Marriage,' said Richard Harris charmingly, 'is a custom brought about by women who then proceed to live off men and destroy them, completely enveloping them in destructive cocoons, or eating away like a poisonous fungus on a tree.' But he insisted that he adored the female of the species.

The lesson we can draw from all this is simple. If the celebrities with money, fame and the adoration of the masses can't make a marriage work then perhaps we shouldn't feel too badly about our own one not functioning.

In fact we could take it further and ask if we know anyone whose relationship runs on an even keel. A London statistician recently informed us that out of every 1,000 people, fourteen get married every year and thirteen divorced. The people who divorce more than once knock that figure askew, but you get the basic message: about half the people who say they will love honour and obey until death do they part ... don't.

In yesteryear we blamed the couple – or either one of them. Today, being more 'enlightened' (for which read less libertine) we blame the situation. We say marriage is a dying institution. We say monogamy is monotony. We say bloody anything to get ourselves out of a pickle. What's causing this global crisis? Selfishness probably. Most people expect happiness today without working for it. They think it grows on trees and relationships owe it to them.

Unfortunately relationships owe nobody anything and the more you expect, the less you tend to get. Because marriage is the oldest lottery going, and the cruellest.

No matter how sure you are of your partner on the Big Day, nobody can predict what he'll be like five years down the road. Or what you may be like yourself. Some marriages reach their nadir when the first child arrives. Some deteriorate after the husband gets a demotion at work. Or even a promotion. Or when he turns his head once too often in the street. Or when you do. There are as many reasons as there are breakdowns.

When the breakdowns occur, there seems to be less of a chance of reconciliation than in the last generation. that was a time when people tended to bury their problems, or live with them discreetly. Today we wear them on our sleeves. This isn't to say there weren't thoroughly miserable marriages in such times. There were. But people seem to have had a higher threshold of pain then than now. Neither did they traipse as speedily to the divorce courts. You might well say, why suffer in silence? Agreed. But there are such things as storms in teacups. And we're seeing quite a few of them nowadays.

It's also a fact that there are more dangers to the institution today than ever before – both from within and without. If we accept the fact that, largely speaking, people are morally weaker than they used to be, so is the world around them more tempting. The important thing to bear in mind is that there's no such phenomenon as a perfect relationship.

If we accept that and don't hold out for ten out of ten how many can we reasonably expect – six? eight? Maybe we should be more conservative and be content with five. If you look for a nine you might end up with a two. There are those who would say if you only have five you should get out. And there are those who do get out – more than once. Often they find themselves making that dodgy odyssey from frying pan into the fire. Statistics also tell us their children, if they have any, have a habit of following a similar behaviour pattern.

It's not that I'm against divorce in theory. Above everything else I believe in people's right to be happy. I also – like most people – know too many people who are in dire emotional states simply because of the absence of divorce. But then I also know people who wouldn't be happy in any relationship – and usually they don't like to be reminded of that fact. Those people are generally adept at seeing the mote in other people's eyes.

There are no magic answers to the above problems, but in the broad scheme of things I seem to see less healthy attitudes in couples than when I was a child. Either I was a very myopic child or there's something seriously wrong with what people want today, or how they're getting it. It's all very well to talk of separation as a panacea but is what's happening in America, or beginning to happen in England the answer?

However if divorce is totally unavoidable you may wish to know about a company whose name roughly translates as 'Transport Service for Troubled People' in Osaka, Japan. They specialise in after-dark moves for wives who want to leave their husbands without alerting the neighbours and before their husbands come home from late-night dinners. I wonder if they're in the Yellow Pages?

The aftermath

*It's difficult to know who gives a woman more pleasure:
the minister who marries or the judge who divorces.*
(Mary Little)

Okay, so it's all over now, baby blue. Your partner has flown
the coop and taken the house, the cat, the kids and not only
that but your fave Robbie Williams CDs as well. 'I do' has
turned to 'Adieu' and suddenly you're sorry you didn't listen
to your mother when she said you were making a big mistake. Why didn't you sign a pre-nup? Or at least notice
something was coming in the post with strange perfumy
smells on the envelopes.

So what to do next? In days gone by you could cry on the
shoulder of a friend, a sibling or even a priest. But now
nobody wants to know. Oh brave new world that has such
people in it. The best you can do is look up the phone book
for an analyst who'll charge through the nose for you to
unload onto him and then offer you a tissue at the end of an
hour with the words 'I'm afraid your time is up. See you next
week'.

Alternatively, you could go on one of those TV shows
where 'experts' (read wallies who have spent a fortnight
studying marital breakdown at a Polytech evening course)
tell you Where It All Went Wrong. They'll bring on someone
else in your position and allow the two of you to play verbal
tennis for a while before they come in with their summa-
tion of where it went down the pan in the last ten minutes
of emotional striptease.

The lady chairing the show might even trot out a
'Famous Author' who's written a book that's selling like hot

cross buns at a funfair with a title like *Why Women Love Men Who Hate Women* or *I'm OK, You're OK, But He Isn't*. It went to the top of the best seller list stateside and then he went on *Jerry Springer* to promote it but unfortunately a row broke out in the course of the show and the trailer park trash jerk with the weight problem who was having it off with his mother's younger sister who was actually younger than him hit Springer over the head with it at the point when a member of the audience suggested the child his aunt was pregnant with mightn't be his at all but rather that of the gay ice hockey player from Idaho who was having secret trysts with her at the local deli every other Thursday.

The said author tells you your should have 'interfaced' more substantively with you partner – which you think (when translated into English) means that you should have had a barney. He also thinks you should have 'squared up to your difficulties in the seminal stages', 'butted out when things got rough' and 'got out of his face every time he went ballistic'. As for now, you need to 'move on', stop being 'hostile' and maybe 'do the God thing' or else before you know it you'll 'need help' which in America invariably means you go back to see the shrink. (You see, you've already had your money's worth, we've already advised that and we haven't even put you through a humiliating televised circus yet.)

Before he goes off the show he'll tell you to check out his other bestsellers: *Men Who Cheat, Women Who Love Men Who Love Men, Men Who Love Women Who Love Men Who Cheat*. Followed by a brief promo on his next book which he intends to attack in his split-level Santa Barbara duplex when he's finished touring. It's going to be his masterpiece – *Men Who Cheat On Women Who Love Men Who Cheat on Women Who Love Men*.

If you actually live in America yourself, you might be interested in going on *Springer*, even at the risk of a few lost clumps of hair. While it may be the only show where the host should consider applying for danger money, this practice seems to have a very therapeutic effect on the contestants. I would recommend it heartily, so long as they replace said clumps of hair in roughly the same position, or make suitable arrangements for cut-price toupees.

The other benefit of going on *Springer* is that it opens your eyes to certain romantic parameters you mightn't have envisaged. Thus, you're likely to be paired with somebody

---

The only time my wife and I had simultaneous orgasms was when the judge signed the divorce papers.
(Woody Allen)

---

who gets off on sucking their lover's toes or pouring candle-wax on their partner's nether regions to the backdrop of a Mozart symphony. Personally I believe we can trace many of these developments back to Bernardo Bertolucci's *Last Tango in Paris* where Marlon Brando found an entirely novel use for butter. This was about the time he began putting on weight and he was probably willing to go to any lengths to get fatty substances out of his fridge. Maria Schneider must be deeply grateful to his dietician for such an approach.

Springer is rather old-fashioned now so if you've got an unusual situation (like 'My best friend's aunt is a transvestical sadomasochist who fantasises about Zen Buddhists') you might prefer to check out some of the more 'liberal' shows. It would be a shame to suffer in silence when there are so many avenues out there to air your grievances and, as the Americans also like to say,' get your life back'.

A fifty-fifty marriage

Divorce is not necessarily the answer, however. It's messy and complicated and you may not wish to drag your private life through the courts. If this is the case you may find this story pretty interesting. A man from Sussex had been at loggerheads with his wife for many moons. They both still live under the same roof, but it's not exactly getting along famously. In fact, not to put a tooth in it, apparently they would like to gouge each other's eyes out if there wasn't the law to contend with.

He did try to kick her out some time ago, but she came back when the money ran out. So they have come up with an ideal situation. A builder friend came up with a novel way of cutting through the tension by building a wall smack in the centre of the house. Personally I think this is an ingenious solution to marital squabbles. He gets half, she gets half: what could be simpler? Admittedly things get a bit dodgy as far as shared use of the kitchen is concerned as he has to dive out of a window to boil the kettle, and neither is the architecture exactly aesthetic, but it's got style.

In fact the next time I have an argy-bargy with She-Who-Must-Be-Obeyed, I'm thinking of investing in a cement mixer and rolling up my sleeves in like fashion. It won't exactly do any favours for my new shagpile carpet in the kitchen-cum-livingroom, I realise and I can't see myself being overjoyed at the prospect of legging it over the kohlrabi patch every time I feel like a cuppa, but it's a lot cheaper than shelling out mega-bucks to a divorce lawyer.

However I'm still wondering as to how they divided up the marital bed. And who gets the en-suite loo? It could cause a few raised eye-brows if he was spied shinnying down the ivy at 4 a.m. in search of somewhere to answer a call of nature.

To pee or not to pee, that is the question …

Tips for a successful divorce

Marriage is only for a little while. It's alimony that lasts forever.

(Quentin Crisp)

He: Make it slow so you have time to hide your money.
She: Make it fast so he doesn't.

He: Make up lots of lies to make her look bad in court.
She: Make up lots of lies to make him look bad in court.

He: Let her have the kids unless you're a New Man.
She: Only let him have the kids if he doesn't want them.

He: Make sure you break all her Madonna CDs.
She: Make sure you break all his golf clubs.

He: Tell all your friends she's cheating on you.
She: Tell all your friends he beats you.

He: Stalk her to make sure she isn't cheating on you.
She: Visit him every night. If he's alone remind him of what he's missing and shout 'loser' in through the window.

He: Have a party to celebrate: you're not losing a wife, you're gaining your freedom.
She: Go to his party to ruin it, put poison in his coffee after forging a suicide note in his writing (after all it wouldn't be the first time you've forged his signature would it?).

The triumph of optimism over reality

I believe in large families. Every woman should have at least three husbands.

(Zsa Zsa Gabor)

If the divorce is working about as well as the marriage, i.e. you're tired, lonely and spending too much time in the office, you may be tempted back into the ring for another go at the jump. In a latterday romance however you have to be just as careful, if not more so, than you were in your carefree youth. Time was when the earth moved, maybe now it's the false teeth or perhaps the padded bra.

If you're still not deterred, but have no idea how to find the next 'special friend' then in this modern age there's a trendy and quirky phenomenon called (usually in a low whisper) The Lonelyhearts Ad.

Three types of people tend to advertise here: Single, Divorced or Widowed. The latter group would appear to be the straightest, if not the most straight-laced. Divorced breeds would, I suppose, tend to be more driven – they've acted on the situation rather than reacted. And singles? Well, these would seem to range from randy fun-lovers to frustrated no-hopers to cranks or kinkies. Or all four.

Not too many people realise the culture shock involved in putting in an ad of this nature – or even responding to one. In many cases you're going from a situation of sitting by the phone waiting for it to ring (when you do this, as you know, it never does) to having your postman bring you in a barrel-load of letters in one fell swoop. When you've sifted through them all you might well be entitled to see yourself as the King (or Queen) of Sheba – but what's at the end of it? More tears on the pillow? Or wham, bam and not so much as a thank you ma'am?

Getting down to the sheer statistics of the matter, a woman who advertises will tend to get four or five times as many replies as a man. This seems about right, considering four or five times as many men as women advertise. According to researchers, men are willing to travel up to 50 miles in one evening to meet a woman they've only spoken to over the phone, often without having seen a photograph. Adventurousness or desperation? Who can say.

The traditional 'wisdom' is that lonelyheart advertisers are either 'ugly, moronic or have chronic personality disorders'. Many people would prefer to cry into their Horlicks in a tatty bedsit than be reduced to it. From a purely sociological point of view, though, more people are alone now than ever were before. Divorce has quadrupled worldwide in the last twenty years. Single people who advertise are often too fed up with a stultified social scene, too cosy with an established relationship, getting out of a relationship, bored, or wanting to go a bit closer to the edge.

Three groups of people have been noted to make out like bandits from divorce. First off, of course, are the solicitors; then the estate agents, and finally dating agencies. There's even a healthy logic to this: statisticians tell us divorced women are three times more likely to die early than married women, and are also more likely to suffer depression, mental illness or even attempt suicide. These dangers could certainly explain why in 1985 in the UK 32% of all marriages were remarriages.

In 1987 *Time Out* ran 13,000 lonely hearts ads. Between them, *Time Out*, *Singles* and *Private Eye* ran a total of 30,000 dates per week – one and a half million per year.

Like everything else, such ads aren't what they used to be. In fact there's more than one League of Decency which would like them censored, or covered in black paint. They tend to range from the mildly amusing ('Noble Savage Man Friday Seeks Lady Crusoe') to imaginative ('Ageless Male, Weary of Solitary Howling to the Gibbous Moon, Seeks Similar Mate') to the severely upfront ('Bachelor Seeks Woman with all the Qualities of a Good Wife and all the Proclivities of a Whore').

Or how about this for size: 'Banned Elderly Raver Seeks Mobile Toyboy for Fun and Frolics. Come Oil my Engine.' Hardly a retiring flower is she? Neither was the lassie who wrote: 'Elegant Forty-year-old Divorcee, Bored with Middle-aged Men, Seeks Interesting Toyboy to be Stripped, Washed and Brought to her Tent.'

Affair-seekers, according to the kind of people who ought to know about such things, don't succeed. According to a *New Statesman* editor 'Men who want to get their leg-over in the afternoon get very few, if any, replies.' Such men have, in many cases, turned advertising into a kind of art form, experimenting with various 'identities' as the need arises – or, more likely, as their old ones get found out. For 'meaningful relationship' with these ladies, one might read one-night stand. Far better the guy who was direct about wanting his fun and frolics. At least you know where you stand … or lie.

Which brings us neatly to another issue: how carefully to work your ad. Many women have been stung by putting 'physically fit' (which turns men off) instead of 'slim' (which obviously doesn't). Those who put 'professional' run the risk of being deemed fuddy-duddies. A lady who said she was looking for a 'well-built' man got a flood of replies imagining well-builtness referred to only one particular area of their anatomy.

People are also wise to the euphemisms endemic in ads of this sort. 'Cuddly' usually means fat, and 'mature' means old(ish). One woman advertised herself as being 'voluptuous', meaning sensual, but she drew few replies because it was taken that she was flabby and blowsy. The perennial problem is, how do you say in thirty-two words what it took that many years to develop? Or, worse, what happens if you don't live up to your ad in his eyes as your blind date arrives with a tape measure picking holes in your exaggerated vital statistics? You may decide to only show your 'better' side in your photograph. This may prove a difficult thing to maintain as you try to keep one half of your face against the wall on your first encounter.

Gentler and more sensitive souls have found themselves too bashful to describe themselves as pretty, even if they were. Not that the average reader of such an ad would believe it anyway, the purveyors of such mating calls being stigmatised either as wallflowers or plain Janes even before they put pen to paper. As one 'expert' commented: 'In Britain and the USA 90% of females marry at an average of twenty-three, while the average age of a single female advertising in the press is thirty-two. The inference is that the other 10% have missed the boat.' And are, to use that equally abhorrent expression 'on the shelf' (I think I prefer 'not for sale').

A more serious problem with lonelyheart advertising is the fact that, by definition, it wars against any form of natural chemistry or spontaneity in the same way computer dating does. There's an inevitable hedginess and apprehensiveness for those first ten minutes (and potentially hours) of any rendezvous set up like this. Most people have found that the best way to beat it is either by ignoring it or laughing at it. When all is said and done, in any case, both parties are in the same boat so there's no need for embarrassment.

Honesty in the original communication (and a firm handshake) is generally deemed to be the best policy. If you've got two arms, two legs and all your own teeth there's no immediate cause for panic. just hold your nose, mutter to yourself 'I may not be Michelle Pfeiffer but I'm not one of the witches out of Macbeth either' and dive in.

Sometimes, though, you can be too honest. One woman had the experience of an ad man saying to her on the first night 'I'm looking for an attractive lady who can help out in my business … marry me' less than five minutes after sitting down with a G & T at their meeting. Needless to say this was the fast track to endsville.

Then again, if it doesn't work out, so what? The best way to avoid being lonely is not to worry about being lonely – just as they say fear of frigidity is one of the main causes of frigidity. As Edna Ferber put it: 'Being an old maid is rather like drowning – a delightful sensation after you cease to struggle.'

A few caveats, though. By their very nature, personal classified ads conduce to infidelity, so beware. Because all contacts made in this manner are completely confidential, there's practically no way to find out if your partner is double (or even triple or quadruple) dating. It's not only men who have the predatory instinct either. One lady is on record as having received over 1,000 replies to her ads and has met approximately 150 of them. And this is in addition to answering ads placed by men as well. Above all, don't have any truck with photocopied letters – a dead give-away to the wandering heart (or the egomaniac).

Widow-hunters are another breed to be wary of, especially if they're living lavishly on a husband's life insurance and thus easy meat for the unscrupulous gold-digger. And then there was the case of the woman who advertised herself as having a five-year-old son and a man answered the ad who turned out to be a paedophile and sexually abused the child.

Generally speaking, however, meeting people in this way would seem to be infinitely safer than the usual scoundrels you run into in clubland at the dead of night when the lights are down and the defences numbed by a few too many. So get cracking with the biros, ladies. And, please, not too spicy. You'll only encourage them.

Ignoring Rita Mae Brown's 'Computer dating is great: if you're a computer' you could take the other alternative and go to a Dating Agency. When you join one you'll be asked to fill in a questionnaire to match you with your perfect partner.

Personal Details

Name of applicant:

Age:

Health of applicant

You must produce health certificates from a practitioner to include details pertaining to:

Eyes:
Ears:
Nose (snoring – undesirable):
Psychiatric record:
Social disease (real or imagined):

Employment

You must provide full details of:
Present employer:
Position held:
Prospects for the next five years:
Please note: persons under middle management, i.e. at least £40,000 p.a. and a company car should not proceed any further.

Financial situation

Supply details of:
Assets:
Houses:
Bonds:
Stocks:
Land:
Cars:
Cash in hand:
Credit limit:

Liabilities

Ex-wives:
Children under six:

Personal loans:
Alimony:
Payouts:
Mortgages:

Financial details must be accompanied by a statement of earnings for the last three financial years. Police and taxation clearances to be included in triplicate and verified by a Justice of the Peace.

But computer dating doesn't always work, or maybe it works too well. Walter Davis applied to one in order find himself a wife. After going through the memory banks the computer came up with his perfect girl called Ethel Davis – his former wife. He didn't argue with technology and remarried her.

Re-marriage

A woman should marry for love.
And keep marrying until she finds it.

(Zsa Zsa Gabor)

You never know till you throw, do you? I'm sure most people are aware that Mickey Rooney, who waltzed up the aisle no less than eight times, once said he was the only person in the world whose marriage license had 'To Whom it May Concern' written on it. He was positively monogamous compared to one lady called Linda Essex.

Because Linda – and no, this isn't a misprint – has been betrothed no less than twenty-two times. That's right: there must be something really tasty in that wedding cake.

'I had my last one annulled because the rascal tricked me,' she says, referring to one Jesse Chandler, and making the rest of us ponder the wisdom of the old epigram that marrying for the second, never mind the twenty-second time, is a triumph of optimism over experience. I mean, you'd imagine she'd have started vetting her intendeds a bit more guardedly after the first dozen or so, wouldn't you?

The said rascal, in any case, pretended he was loaded, but after they tied the knot she found out his sole income was a measly $427 Social Security disability cheque a month. It's a tough world out there for innocent unsuspecting brides, isn't it? Except in this case the strange thing is that Jesse was Linda's sixteenth husband as well, but presumably he had a job then. A lot can happen, it seems, between six marriages.

At the moment, in any case, Linda has her eyes on a

twenty-third hopeful, so let's keep our fingers crossed shall we? Especially those with rings on them. Above all we must avoid being judgmental about her matrimonial search. The plain fact of the matter is that some people are speedier than others in locating their ideal partner.

However, compared to Scotty Wolfe, Linda is only warming up. Scotty has been married a record 28 times. And, at the age of eighty-six, he's lined up his next conquest to a fifteen-year-old schoolgirl. He definitely believes in starting them young, doesn't he? His intended is Bernadina Brachmontez, daughter of a local dentist's assistant. Questions could be asked about why a fifteen-year-old would want to marry a wheelchair-bound eighty-six-year-old Baptist minister who lives in a retirement hotel in a remote desert town, whose last marriage ended after only four months. She said 'I want to marry Scotty. I am wearing his diamond ring.' Ah, that explains it then. He has also offered to buy her a computer, give her driving lessons and has wooed her with the prospect of getting on TV because she's marrying so young (which, he incidentally added, 'might earn a $5,000 donation to my church'). You'd think that the Californian TV stations would be used to Scotty's antics by now. After all, bride number twenty-seven was only fourteen!

But while Scotty is making inroads into the adolescent female population, Udaynath Dakhinray, an Indian landowner from Orissa, isn't hanging about and has clocked up a whopping eighty-nine brides. Of his previous eighty-eight, fifty-seven left him and twenty-six died. Dakhinray pledged himself to a life of polygamy after his first wife left him thirty-six years before, after just two weeks. Which just goes to show that experience doesn't necessarily make you wiser.

Zimmer-frame Lotharios

I'm at an age where my back goes out more than I do.
(Phyllis Diller)

How do you know when you're past it?

(1) You get a letter informing you your marriage licence has expired.

(2) You get arrested for a sex offence but when the judge takes a look at you he throws the case out.

(3) The last thing you did by hand was put your finger through the wedding ring.

(4) You're relieved when girls say no.

(5) The wildest get-together you attended in the past twelve months was a coffee morning.

(6) You want to give up your seat for the old lady on the bus ... but can't.

(7) You have a choice of two alternatives and decide on the one that gets you home by 9 p.m.

(8) It takes you all night to do once what you used to do all night.

(9) You're afraid to bend down to tie your shoelaces in case you can't get up.

(10) You feel like the morning after but you haven't had the night before.

(11) Your weightlifting now consists of standing up.

(12) Your pacemaker is on steroids.

(13) A publisher asks you to write a book called *In Bed with the Enemy*.

I asked my husband to restore my confidence. I told him my boobs were gone, my stomach was gone, and asked him to say something nice about my legs.
'Blue goes with everything', he said.
(Joan Rivers)

Afterthought: The Rendezvous

The more I see of men, the more I admire dogs.
(Brigitte Bardot)

It's the nightmare scenario. The relationship is over, finished, kaput. The problem is you're not quite over him and now you run into him in the street. The conversation will run like this ...

She: Hello. (Oh God, not him)

He: Hiyah! (Damn, she saw me. Now I'm trapped!)

She: I was just thinking about you last week. (I was hoping you might have emigrated.)

He: And me about you – you look great. (Jesus, she's really starting to show her age.)

She: You too. (He must have been out on the town last night.) How are things?

He: Great. (Until I met you). And you? (She asked, so I better.)

She: Fantastic. (I've only taken two overdoses since I saw you last)

                         NERVOUS PAUSE

She: Are you still living in that quaint little house? (I always hated the dive.)

He: Actually I've just bought a new place. (And we're second-mortgaged up to the eyeballs.)

She: That's lovely. You must be over the moon. (I always knew he was a closet yuppie.)

He: Thrilled to bits. So is Denise. (Actually she said she'd divorce me unless we moved to a bigger place.)

She: How is Denise? (The bitch. The two of you deserve each other.)

He: OK. she keeps asking after you. (And gets a lift if I give her some bad news.)

She: That's nice of her. Tell her I'd love to meet her. (I've always hated her guts ever since she stole you off me all those years ago.)

He: Will do. (How she'll laugh at that one).

ANOTHER NERVOUS PAUSE

She: So that's the way. (Oh my God, what am I going to say next?)

He: You're looking great anyway. (Shit, I said that before.)

She: It must be the clean living. (I hit the sack at 5 a.m. this morning.)

He: How are things in the job? (She always had about as much ambition as a pea.)

She: Brilliant. I just got promoted. (Demoted, actually.)

He: Delighted to hear it. (She's probably on protective notice as we speak.)

She: At least it means I can afford a decent summer holiday for once in my life. (I'm going to Butlins again.)

He: It's not a bit more than you deserve. (She's probably going to Butlins again.)

She: How about yourself – where are you off to this year? (With that new mortgage I'll probably run into him.)

He: Oh, anywhere the fancy takes me. I don't like to plan too much in advance. (I can see by her face she knows I'm lying through my teeth.)

She: Tightlipped as ever! (Cute hoor.)

He: I'll send you a postcard. (Like hell.)

ANOTHER SLIGHTLY LONGER NERVOUS PAUSE

She: Oh God, look at the time. I'd better fly. (I haven't got a thing on all day but this conversation is boring me out of my tree.)

He: Me too. (Liar) Listen, we must meet up sometime. (Please don't say yes.)

She: I'd love to. You have my number, don't you? (If

there's a God in heaven I'm now formally begging for it to be lost.)

He: Of course. (It's actually at the bottom of the loo.)

She: Great, it's up to you then. (Relief! Off the hook!)

He: I'll give you a raincheck next week. (Do you believe pigs fly?)

She: I'll be waiting by the phone. (If I pick it up and it's him it will suddenly become, er, sort of banjaxed.)

He: Maybe we could take in a show. (I can't believe I'm saying this.)

She: What could be nicer. (Except a slow painful death.)

He: Well, see you then. (Free, at last.)

She: Best of luck. (Looking on the bright-side, maybe a juggernaut will run him over.)

The End?